THE TRAVEL JOURNALS OF TAPPAN ADNEY
VOL. 1, 1887-1890

Edwin Tappan Adney,
Riley Brook, Tobique, September, 1896

THE TRAVEL JOURNALS OF
TAPPAN ADNEY
Vol. 1, 1887-1890

REVISED EDITION

EDITED BY C. TED BEHNE

GOOSE LANE

Edited by Paula Sarson.
Cover illustration by E. Tappan Adney.
Cover design by Jaye Haworth.
Page design by Jaye Haworth and Chris Tompkins.
Printed in Canada.
10 9 8 7 6 5 4 3 2 1

Library and Archives Canada Cataloguing in Publication

Adney, E. Tappan (Edwin Tappan), 1868-1950, author
The travel journals of Tappan Adney. Vol. 1, 1887-1890 / edited by C. Ted
Behne. -- Revised edition.

Includes bibliographical references and index.
ISBN 978-0-86492-887-0 (paperback)

1. Adney, E. Tappan (Edwin Tappan), 1868-1950--Travel--New Brunswick.
2. Adney, E. Tappan (Edwin Tappan), 1868-1950--Travel--Nova Scotia.
3. Adney, E. Tappan (Edwin Tappan), 1868-1950--Diaries.
4. New Brunswick--Description and travel. 5. Nova Scotia--Description and travel.
6. Malecite Indians. I. Behne, C. Ted, 1942-2014, editor II. Title.

FC2467.3.A46 2016   917.15'1043   C2015-908273-0

We acknowledge the generous support of the Government of Canada,
the Canada Council for the Arts, and the Government of New Brunswick.

Nous reconnaissons l'appui généreux du gouvernement du Canada,
du Conseil des arts du Canada, et du gouvernement du Nouveau-Brunswick.

Goose Lane Editions
500 Beaverbrook Court, Suite 330
Fredericton, New Brunswick
CANADA E3B 5X4
www.gooselane.com

RECYCLED
Paper made from
recycled material
FSC® C103567

CONTENTS

7   Preface to the Revised 2016 Edition

9   Foreword

11   Introduction

17   First Trip to New Brunswick, 1887-1889

     65   A Trip in a Birch Canoe through the Squatook Lakes, Sept. 24, 1888

     87   Caribou Hunt to Ayers Lake with Peter Joe and Hum Sharp, Christmas 1888

     99   Second Caribou Hunt to Nackawick and Guimac, January 1889

     109   Snowshoes

123   Second Trip to New Brunswick and First Trip to Nova Scotia, Summer of 1890

139   Acknowledgements

141   Notes

153   Index

PREFACE TO THE REVISED 2016 EDITION

When *The Travel Journals of Tappan Adney, 1887-1890* was first published in 2010, it was warmly received by an audience keen to learn more about this fascinating character and his early adventures in New Brunswick and Nova Scotia. Its success encouraged us to publish a second volume of Tappan Adney's journals in 2014, *The Travel Journals of Tappan Adney, Vol. 2, 1891-1896*. Based on feedback from readers of the first volume, as well as our own experience, we refined our approach to the second, with a little more rigorous editing (which sometimes meant letting Tappan Adney's errors stand) and a cleaner and more reader-friendly presentation. Now, we have decided to revise the first volume to match the standards of the second.

For the revised edition, we went back to Adney's original typescript and compared our published version. Between transcription of the hundred-year-old text into electronic word-processing files, editing, and book design, some errors inevitably crept into the final document. We have corrected as many of these errors as we could find, while also relaxing our editorial hand when it came to Tappan Adney's idiosyncratic style. Some minor errors of spelling or punctuation, where needed for clarity, have been corrected silently, and the occasional interpolation of a word or remark on illegible text appears in brackets, but otherwise Adney's unedited voice is given free range.

In James Wheaton's transcription (see Foreword), an excess of scruples led to some slight bowdlerization of the text. Although well-intentioned, these excisions obscure the historical context of Adney's ideas. A product of his time, Adney's language echoes the norms and prejudices of his society, occasionally in terms that are jarring or offensive to modern sensibilities, but the reader never doubts his genuine respect and fondness for the people he describes.

Finally, some discrepancies between the ordering of pages in the archival typescript and the purported dates of certain events (which Adney or some later editor occasionally corrected in pencil on the typescript) suggest that some parts of the journal were bound out of chronological order. We have therefore taken the liberty of moving the section headed "A Trip in a Birch Canoe . . ." from where it followed the "Snowshoes" section in the archive to where it rightly belongs, prior to the "Caribou Hunt to Ayers Lake."

Special thanks are due to Liz Behne for her support and input throughout the publishing history of the journals, and especially during our preparation of this revised edition. We would also like to extend our thanks to Andrea Bear Nicholas and Daryl Hunter, who both assisted Ted in his editing and annotation of the journals and provided editorial guidance advice on the revised edition. Andrea Bear Nicholas also located a couple of images that had been missed on the first go-round, which we are pleased to include. Although Ted Behne passed away in 2014, just as the second volume of these journals was going to press, we owe him a debt of gratitude for his vision and perseverance in bringing Tappan Adney's Maritime journals from the archive to a wide audience.

FOREWORD

Edwin Tappan Adney's "First Trip to New Brunswick" is a book about eight-and-a-half by eleven inches, bound in cardboard with reinforced corners, and fastened with copper staples. The paper he typed on was typical of the time, a watermarked light brown, rather brittle now. He evidently transcribed his handwritten notes at a later date, and even went over the typed version subsequently, adding some headings in red ink and some notes in pencil. His typing was not very good (there are many typos, and often letters, periods, and capital letters are missing), and in his binding process he cut off some of the right edge of the paper such that occasionally part of a word has been lost.

I have done my best to transcribe to the computer what he typed (and what I think he meant to type) and have added notes and a few photographs to provide some background about various people. I have scanned his sketches and maps, which add so much to his story, added a photo taken in 1896, and reproduced the original first page. Tappan Adney, a man whose life bridged the nineteenth and twentieth centuries, used terms common in those days. He refers to the Canadian First Peoples as "Indians" or "injuns," as did most white people at that time.

This journal is significant to a study of the character of Tappan Adney, because in it he first revealed the passion for nature that guided the rest of his life and the experiences of life in the outdoors that enabled him to perform his brilliant reporting of the Klondike Stampede.[1]

James W. Wheaton
September 1999

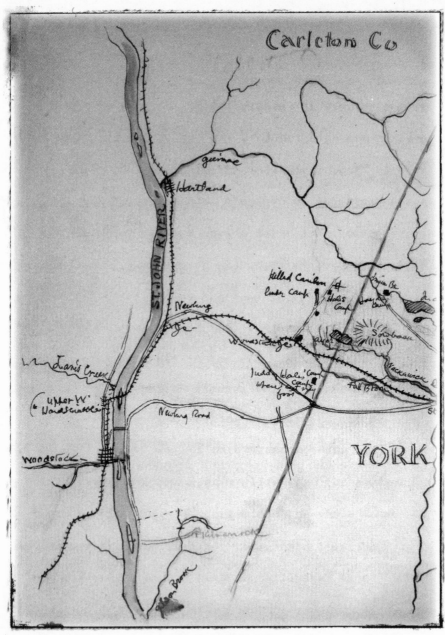

Woodstock area, 1887

INTRODUCTION

When Tappan Adney arrived in Upper Woodstock, New Brunswick, on July 11, 1887, two days before his nineteenth birthday, he planned to spend a month of his summer respite as a guest of the Sharp family. He and his sister Mary Ruth were invited by M.B. Sharp, who lived in Mrs. Adney's boarding house in New York City while studying music and voice.

His valise was loaded with books to study for his entrance exams at Columbia College. He had just completed four years at Trinity School, an exclusive Episcopal prep school in New York whose best graduates went on to Columbia College. Trinity School was then, as it is today, one of the finest secondary schools in the United States, educating its students in classical literature (in the original Latin and Greek), history, the natural sciences, world geography, mathematics, English literature, and French.

But Adney's college plans were forgotten when he came under the spell of New Brunswick's outdoors life. This bookish young man was utterly transformed by the allure of New Brunswick's wilderness and the Native people he found there. His brief summer vacation became a twenty-month sojourn that inspired and guided the rest of his life. This journal, and three others covering his first trips to New Brunswick and Nova Scotia, chronicle his first observations and experiences as he discovered his new world. [1]

His life up to that point had been a prelude, an academic rehearsal, for the real-world classroom in which he would study thereafter. His mother, a capable, self-reliant woman with strong Episcopalian beliefs, had brought him and his sister to New York four years before, in 1883, to take advantage of the city's superior educational opportunities. In the mid-1880s, New York City was the fastest growing city in the world, expanding by sixty thousand people each year. It was the financial and cultural capital of America and the country's largest and most modern city. It served as a living laboratory for Adney, providing both formal and informal education opportunities, as well as friendships with amateur and professional scientists who lived and worked there.

His passion then was ornithology, the study of birds. During the warm-weather months, he would go at dawn to Central Park to observe them. The park was an ideal birdwatching venue, situated below one of the continent's major flyways for migrating birds. He had opportunities to study both resident birds and semi-annual transients.

He was a night student for three years at the Art Students League of New York, a revolutionary art school formed by students and run by them in protest against the regimented, formal curriculum of traditional art schools. His instructors were among the most celebrated American artists of his day, including William Merritt Chase, the school's chief instructor. Adney's class sketches and paintings attest to both his talent and skill.

Young Adney had lived in a few different places before he arrived in New York. He was born in Athens, Ohio, on July 13, 1868, where his father worked as a professor at Ohio University. At age five Adney moved with his family to Washington, Pennsylvania, where his father became a member of the faculty of Washington and Jefferson College. At age eleven, Adney moved again with his family to Pittsboro, North Carolina, where they purchased a tobacco farm, which they sharecropped for income while Adney's father searched for a teaching job. As a boy he was home-schooled by his father, who specialized in tutoring new students struggling with college-level work. At a time when public schools were non-existent and private education was available only to the children of wealthy families, Adney was given personal instruction from his father in the natural sciences, mathematics, history, geography, English literature, and Latin. He was an exceptionally precocious student who, at age thirteen, was admitted to the University of North Carolina at Chapel Hill and attended successfully for two years carrying a full academic course load.

Adney's journals are not diaries or daily records, but rather periodic accounts of experiences and reflections that he found noteworthy. They were typed from his handwritten copy decades later, sometimes with typographical errors or with blanks (reproduced as three em dashes: ———) for dates or names that he perhaps intended to add later. He added interpretive commentary, looking back with the perspective of time and life experience, and bound them in booklet form, most likely between 1933 and 1946.

As much as possible, the original text has been kept intact. Adney came to New Brunswick from the United States, so his spelling reflects his origins. Although Adney acknowledges that the spelling "Malicete" was in use at the time, he uses the older Milicete. Both are precursors to the spelling we see today: Maliseet. Adney uses Nackawick Settlement and Nackawick for what is today spelled Nackawic, and Squatook Lakes in Quebec for what is today spelled Squatec Lakes. Due to fluctuations in spelling, Saint John River has been standardized in keeping with current government-sanctioned spelling.

In addition, despite Jim Wheaton's diligent efforts, there are instances in his transcription where he misinterpreted Adney's casually typed and faded manuscript. "Barn swallow," for example, is actually "bank swallow" on closer examination and "Sp———" turns out to be "spruce." A handwritten section on snowshoes that was omitted from Jim Wheaton's transcription has been restored here in an effort to faithfully reproduce Adney's original intent.

Also, to provide historical context and to clarify otherwise obscure references in Adney's text, numerous endnotes have been added. Captions have been provided by the editor, except for Adney's originals, which are marked as such in the list of illustrations.

These journals allow us to share Adney's discoveries as we join him on his first-trip adventures. They take us back to a time, long past, when New Brunswick still had abundant wilderness and wildlife. They are filled with descriptions of real people, places, and events, and are illustrated with sketches and remarkably accurate maps.

The stories he heard around campfires and his own novice experiences with hunting, fishing, and camping became savory ingredients for the outdoor adventure articles he later wrote and illustrated for New York–based magazines in the 1890s. Reflecting on his first trips, he wrote, "Nothing had a more positive influence upon my life. . . . It determined the whole manner of my later life, and later when [I] set to earn a livelihood, it supplied the experience that [was] of the greatest service to me. . . . Here was a whole new world thrown open, a kind of air I had never breathed before."

His fascination with New Brunswick was not only life-changing for him, but also for the Native people who befriended him. He became perhaps the best non-Native friend the Native people of New Brunswick ever had. His monumental canoe book, *The Bark Canoes and Skin Boats of North America*, allowed Native and non-Native canoe builders to reconstruct traditional Maliseet birchbark canoes long after this important part of Maliseet material culture had become dormant. Adney was a fluent speaker of the Maliseet language. For more than fifteen years he worked with his friend Dr. Peter Paul, of the Woodstock First Nation, to develop what would have become the largest and most comprehensive Maliseet dictionary and grammar if it had been published. Adney had a significant advantage with this dictionary because his collaborator, Dr. Paul, was raised by his grandparents, so the Maliseet he learned as a child was a generation older and less diluted than all of his contemporaries.

Adney was infamous in the Woodstock area for his eccentricities, which included walking through the nature trails on his property with careless disregard for his clothing, or lack of it, while "talking" with birds and squirrels. In his linguistics research, he used food, as well as sounds the animals themselves make — much like some vocalizations of the Maliseet language — to literally charm birds and squirrels out of the trees to eat from his hands and perch on his shoulders. It would have been easy, if you didn't know him, to dismiss him as a crazy old hermit who thought he could talk with animals. His friend Dr. Fred Clarke, a prolific author of fiction and non-fiction books about life in New Brunswick, knew better. He called him "the most remarkable genius I have ever known."

In 1946, Peter Paul was arrested and charged with theft of natural resources from the property of the white land owner. Paul's defense was that he was entitled, by ancient treaty with the British, to continue his traditional lifestyle, which included harvesting natural resources from the forest or wherever he could find them. Adney agreed with him and found a copy of the treaty to use in Paul's defense. In so doing, he became the first person to attempt to present a well-documented treaty-entitlement defense of a Native person in a Canadian court. Despite his eccentric reputation, he was an intellectual giant whose mind was formidable when focused. The judge respected this about him. Before Adney could present his argument, the judge adjourned the case to await the return of the Indian agent whose responsibility it was to hire a "real" lawyer to defend Peter Paul. The prosecuting attorney wrote Adney a personal note saying how disappointed he was that he wouldn't have the intellectual challenge of arguing the case against him.

After his life was redirected by the impact of that first trip to New Brunswick, Adney went on to great achievements and profound disappointments. He was a complex, difficult man and a bundle of contradictions. He had a genius-level intellect and prodigious artistic skills but struggled most of his life to simply pay his bills. He was the son of a college professor, home-schooled, and attended college at an early age, but he never graduated. He was respected as an equal by the leading anthropologists and ethnologists of his day but couldn't get a job in either field because he lacked academic credentials. His collection of 110 model birchbark canoes, now held by the Mariners' Museum in Newport News, Virginia, is priceless today, but he was penniless when he died.

He lived to be eighty-two, and when he died in October 1950, he left behind a vast legacy of artwork, magazine articles, books, bark canoe models, heraldry, Native ethnology and linguistics papers, and his tireless work as a champion of Native rights in the Maritime provinces.

In this, and his other journals, we have a glimpse of him as a young man, full of promise and excitement, eagerly anticipating the new life he was just beginning. It was the life chronicled in the pages of this journal that first became evident to him at age nineteen in Upper Woodstock, New Brunswick, where he ultimately spent his last days, surrounded by the woods and people he had come to love.

C. Ted Behne
June 2010

First Trip

TO

NEW BRUNSWICK:

Fr. June 30, 1887, - Feb. 28, '89

TOGETHER WITH

First Trip to NOVA SCOTIA, & Second Trip to New BRUNSWICK, July to Nov, 1890.

From New York to Woodstock

The day that school[1] closed, at five o'clock in the afternoon of the 30th of June, 1887, I started by the Fall River boat[2] with the intention ultimately of reaching the town of Woodstock, situated in western New Brunswick, on the Saint John River, where I had friends whom I was going to pay a visit. My chief interest in life at that time was centered in the study of ornithology and all my notes of that time, whether of travel or the people I met, bore in some way on the study of birds.

It was only gradually, as my horizon widened, that I came to have that larger interest in nature and nothing did more to direct in broader channels a strong love of nature, and nothing had a more positive influence upon my life than the journey on which I was now setting out. It determined the whole manner of my later life, and later when [I] set to earn a livelihood, it supplied the experience that has been, and will ever be, of the greatest service to me. It furnished me the inspiration and it continues to do so now. Though I little knew it then, fortunate [it] was that I saw the woods as I did, experiences full of hardships and discouragements, but in an unconventional way.

***

The berth was hot and unendurable. There were great crowds of people traveling at that season, so I went out and went to sleep on a coil of rope on the deck of the steamer. Arrived Boston in the early morning, breakfast in the Old Colony station, and a cab to the International Steamship Co and took a berth for Saint John, via Portland and Eastport.

The sea was like glass, but for the long ground swell, and the petrels circled around on the smooth surface like swallows. Some women on the hurricane deck; my field glasses were in evidence: "distinge"[3] perhaps. One of the women whispered to the other, "I wish we had brought our opera glasses along." Finally, curiosity getting the better, she asked to borrow them; when she had done which, she could not focus them and politely as I could, I had to show her how. Why is it when people see someone else with something that is nice, [they] must always try to let that person know they have the same themselves? Only in this case their vanity gave them a sad fall.

At Portland I went ashore and all I noted of Portland [was] its magnificent shade trees which were then harboring the following species of birds: red-eyed vireo, chipping sparrow, and redstart, all in full song.

Early the next morning, as we steamed eastward, the rugged, uninviting, rocky coast of Maine came into view and later the cliffs of Grand Manan appeared on the right. Entering Eastport between Campobello and the mainland, the waters were crowded with vast flocks of a small gull larger than terns. In thousands they covered the surface of the water darting hither and thither in pursuit of small fish. Where their white wings cut against the dark shores of Campobello, the air quivered like a swarm of bees. The two hours in the quaint down east town of Eastport I spent in getting as far out of town as possible, and my journal records a list of fourteen birds, the only notable fact being the nest of a Maryland yellowthroat in a fir bush two and one-half feet from the ground, instead of on the ground.

On the dock, some boys were lying flat on their bellies catching flounders and pollock in the clear green waters. One could see the fish, a foot long, take hold of the hook, and if a sculpin came along and tried to seize the bait, the boys would jerk the hook away. Now and then one managed to get hold and then they banged it off [on] a post and you would think they were dead, but when they struck the water they were as lively as ever. One could see fifteen feet down.

We reached Saint John at three o'clock, the 3rd of July. One thing I had not figured on, the good people of the province do not do anything wicked on Sunday. It was Saturday. The boat was late and I had missed

Fishing off the wharf at Eastport [Maine]

the last train till Monday. I went at once to the Royal[4] and then took letters to Mr. Montague Chamberlain[5] and at his earnest and certainly most kind solicitation went as a guest to his home.

The next day was Sunday, and while the others went to church like good people, I took to the woods, or what I could find on the rocky shores of the Bay of Fundy. It was the hottest day that I have any distinct recollection of, and I came back wilted as I never have been before or since. But I got a fine list of birds, some of which were old friends met with for the first time in their summer homes. That was the charm of the study of bird life. I knew them all as migrants or winter visitants. That night we called on Banks the oologist[6]. He is a blacksmith, but no common man. He showed us his unique find of the Cape May warbler's nest and the second recorded nest of the bay-breasted warbler. He had just got back from a jaunt and he gave me a fresh set of four newly-found eggs of the sharp-shinned hawk that he had got out of the top of a spruce tree, and a fresh set of savannah sparrow eggs.

Monday, July 4 An excursion of the Natural History Society [from New York City] to Meagone Island [*sic*: likely Manawagonish Island] in the Bay of Fundy off Saint John. Thirty of us went along in two small yachts. Meagone Island [is] a rocky island covered with dense, stunted spruce and a small clearing where some sheep were browsing. Dense fog swept in, enveloping all things with reeking, dripping moisture, shutting out all things but the tinkle of a sheep bell, the murmuring of the waves on the beach, and the voices of a few hardy birds. Strong, clear, like a flute in the hands of a master, the hermit thrush — a pathos that is known to no other bird. There is no song of more pure beauty, and one must come here or listen in the early morn in some far New Brunswick wilderness, to hear this, the most beautiful of bird music. I found the nest, containing four blue-green eggs, on the ground, among the cool, damp mosses and luxuriant ferns. The fog was so thick we could hardly find our way back to the harbor.

July 5 An early walk with Mr. Chamberlain and noted three new species of birds. It was marvelous to me how Chamberlain could identify from a single note that [which] would have escaped me altogether.

July 6 Mr. Chamberlain was to give a lecture before the Society and wanted some fresh birds, so I went out back of the city and found myself in wild woods. I poked about in a dense cedar swamp. The usual fog came in. I lost my bearings and walked in a circle until I remembered that the wind was probably constant. Then I took a course by the wind and got out. Thankfully, I got a crow for the lecture.

July 8 Took passage aboard a small side-wheel steamer, the *David Weston* for Fredericton up the river. Next morning, arrived at the capital. I met on the steamer a young Mr. Goodridge Roberts,[7] whom I afterward met at the house of his brother, Prof. Charles G.D. Roberts[8] at Windsor, Nova Scotia.

I sketched the curious wood boats, two-masted schooners with tremendous sheer forward, loaded on deck with deals[9] so that the hulls of the boats were actually submerged, all but the high nose of the bow. They came down wing-and-wing under a northwest breeze. Going back, it is said they make better time than the steamer. Here at Fredericton were the booms with their enormous quantities of logs from up river.

There was a tall bank of sawdust several miles below the city, and I went there and found hundreds of bank swallows nesting in the face of the heap, which was as hard and firm as a bank of sand. I got several sets of eggs.

I made another ghastly error. I had forgotten about the no-Sunday-train business, and so, instead of going on to Woodstock, only fifty miles away, I had a wearisome wait at the Queen Hotel.

Monday, July 11 Arrived at Woodstock and walked with my valise to Upper Woodstock. On the way, inquired for the Sharps'[10] house, and was told to keep on till I came to the most remarkable house I had ever seen.[11]

My sister[12] was at the Sharps', and I received a warm welcome from them all.

I had brought books along to study for the rest of my entrance examination at Columbia, namely Xenophon[13] and Ancient Geography. I had truly meant to study conscientiously, but here was a whole new world thrown open, a kind of air that I had never breathed before. Why, one could no more study than a deer could or a wild Injun. Not that we were in the woods, but we were so near there, in the oldest settlements, that one had but to go half a mile back to find traces of an original forest that are now as wild looking as any that one will find in the remotest wilderness. No woods had ever impressed [me]

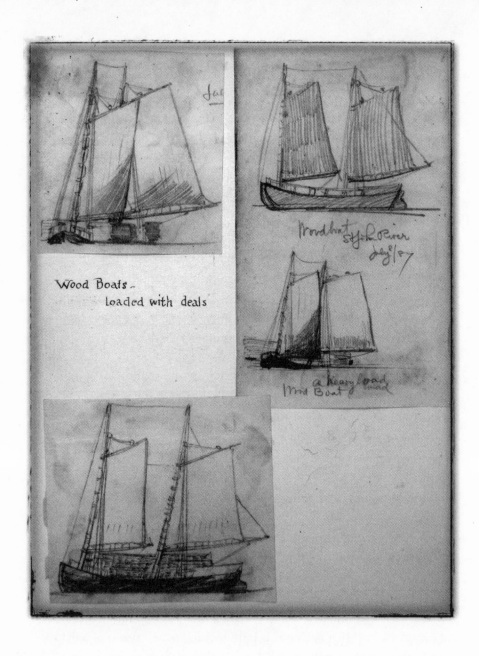

Wood Boats -
        loaded with deals

Woodboat StJohn R River
    July 87

a heavy load
Mud Boat

Indian Encampment, Upper Woodstock, New Brunswick, 1887-1888;
inset: Milicete Summer Camp, Upper Woodstock, NB
(Peabody Essex Museum Neg. No. 32077)

as these woods did. Only a short way from the house was an Indian encampment with their birchbark houses on the point made by Lane's Creek and the river. Here, during the summer, they made birch canoes, and I got to know them all well: old Peter Joseph and John Solis.

They took a fancy to me, and I took a fancy to them, and they taught me many things: how to build canoes, and Peter Joe took me with him into the woods when he got the bark to make canoes, and I made small ones of my own, exact models. One of these models is in the Museum of Natural History at New York, a 1/5 scale;[14] the other is now owned by Mr. Allison Connell of Woodstock (got this back; since stolen).

Milicete[15] Bird Names

Having an intense interest in birds, my first thought was to get a list of the bird names of these Indians, and so I set out on a work of love, and prepared a list of the Bird Names of the Milicete Indians, the first ever published, read before the Linnaean Society[16] of New York, together with some animal names. I picked up some more of the language, but I did not know the proper way to go at it, until it was too late to get [it] all.

These Indians are of the tribe called Milicetes, but that is only the corruption of a name by which they are known to the Micmacs of the eastern part of the Province and Nova Scotia. The Micmac name is Mali-zĭt-ʼe-watc (sing. Mal-zĭt-ʼdjĭk). Their own name is Wūl-ās-tuk-wĭ-ûk, or People of the "Wallastook" or Saint John River. They are found in several villages along the river, notably above Fredericton, and at the mouth of the Tobique. They have strong affinities with the Passamaquoddies. They regard themselves as distinct from the Penobscots, but they assimilate with them at Old Town and Mattawamkeag [both in Maine]. They are wholly distinct from the Micmacs. The others can understand each other's language, but Micmac is not intelligible to the others, though I have heard an intelligent Micmac say by close attention he could get the sense. The roots of the language are the same.

The Milicetes remember their old enemies the Mohawks, and they have stories of that time which some say took place five hundred years ago, notably how the raft of Mohawks [was] taken over the Grand Falls of the Saint John by a captured Milicete squaw, whom one story says went over with the raft; whom another version says swam ashore. And other such stories.

They used playfully to call me the Mohawk or Ktchee Mohawk, "Big Mohawk," from my tallness, and when I got the intonation or the "genius" of their manner of talking, they would exclaim, "All you got do marry squaw then just same one Ninjun." I came in time by diligent inquiry from many different persons to acquire a more extensive knowledge of their bird names than any one Indian had. I had a serious illustration of this when on a later trip in the woods with old Ambrose Lockwood. Ambrose gave me the name of a bird, giving the English name and asked me what the Indian name was for it.

Besides the above-mentioned reservations there are others at different points. In fact, the Canadian policy has been always to break up the tribes into small reservations, allowing the Indians to keep any particular spot that they were accustomed to. Such places are a convenient bank of the river, generally on a point where a brook or larger stream enters.

They dress as white men do, except they have a weakness for bright cottons of solid colors: greens, orange, etc., and in summer wear moccasins almost altogether. They are the builders of bark canoes, the makers of snowshoes and of baskets, and where they are near such places they make some of the best guides and camp helpers.

In some instances they settle down and acquire houses and work land on a small scale, farming on their reservations, but commonly they wander about a good deal. But to show [how] far civilized ideas prevail, an old squaw wife of a well-to-do man of the Point was telling me about her daughter, who had married a downriver Indian who lived after the old way. She had her daughter come up and live half the year with her, for said she, "I not like have my daughter live that way. That's ole time way."

I stopped in her house, and it was furnished in every respect as well [as], though not unlike, the ordinary country house. There were even tall lamps and a piano. The only Indian part of the house was the kitchen and dining room, which was where the baskets were made, and the floor would be littered a foot deep with shavings. As a general thing, the old squaws do not speak any language but their own. The men speak English more or less well and some know French. They often marry French women, and so the race is losing its pure Indian characteristics. Peter Joe lived with his aged mother and small nephew in a house built of birchbark about ten by fifteen feet square with [a] double shed roof. This was their summer house. In winter they rent warmer abodes.

The Wūl-ās-tuk-wǐ-ûks

Where did they come from? Noel Francis Sapier told me he heard his father tell that a very long time ago, hundreds of years, some eight or ten families came from the westward and settled on the Olastuk.[17] They were pleased with the country and stayed.

Peter Joe thought Noel Sapier was mistaken. "We never did come from the west. Injun always was here, grew up with the country, just the same as moose and caribou."

They take their name from their own river, now called the Saint John. The name Malicete, "Milicete," etc., is the name given by the Micmacs who inhabit the east shore of New Brunswick, Quebec, and Nova Scotia. Nicholas Denys was a Frenchman having a trading post on Cape Breton, and his authority extended as far as Gaspe. The Milicetes have the name as one of their own personal names but they do not know the old Denys (*Conquest of Canada*).[18]

Anciently the Eskimo may have extended far south and mixed with the Milicetes. Today they are mixed with French so that there are very few of the old type of Indian left. They are often well bearded and light in complexion. They do not know any Indians of the name "Wobanaki."[19]

I used to hear stories of the old doings of the Mohawks and there are different versions of these stories. There is much elasticity in dates. The story of how the Indian woman piloted the Mohawks over the Grand Falls I heard as follows from Noel Sapier.

How the Mohawks went over Grand Falls

"A long time ago the Mohawks were great fighters and they came here from the north, up Canada way. They liked the looks of the country so they wanted to take possession of it. There was fighting going on nearly all the time, nearly every year.

"A long time ago, about two three hundred years ago, a war party [of] three hundred Mohawks came down from Canada. Way up river near the head of [the] Olastuk they captured two Indian trappers and their squaws. They scalped both the men. There they built a big raft of cedar logs and started down the river with the two squaws to guide them. It was night and very dark, just before daylight, as they came to the Grand Falls. They were sleeping in rows with feet together and every man had his big toe tied to a small pole at their feet, so if one woke up all the others would feel the jerk and wake up too. The squaws sat in front, one at each corner. A few Mohawks were awake. They were getting near the Grand Falls. When they heard the roaring, they asked the squaws, 'what is that?' The squaws told them, 'That's only rapids you hear.' They reached the wide part of the river just above the falls and there the squaws jumped overboard and finned it for the shore. The raft went over with all the Mohawks.

"Injuns came from down river, everywhere, and they scalped the Mohawks that were drowned. Everybody felt very good."

Noel said that below the falls were some saplings and they nailed the scalps onto these. Then they had a big scalp dance for a month and they wore a trench with their feet around the saplings—it was a deep trench. Noel's father had the trees shown him in his time and they were big old trees.

A Treaty with the Mohawks

"About seventy-five years ago[20] a party of Indians started upriver from down Meductic[21] (Woodstock) to spear salmon. They had ten canoes.

When they came to about thirty miles above Woodstock, they came suddenly onto a big party of Mohawks. They couldn't go on [and] they didn't dare to run. The old men got together. There was a sharp turn in the river there, so they said, 'We will keep on around the bend of the river out of sight.'

"And then they picked up their canoes and carried them overland to a place below and then they came upriver again. The Mohawks were watching them, and when they saw the canoes coming all day they thought there was a big party. They kept on till dark and went into camp there.

"The Mohawks were fooled into thinking there was a great party of Milicetes. Early next morning, the Milicetes saw a single canoe coming from the direction of the Mohawk camp. There was a tomahawk sticking up in the bow. That was a sign of peace. The old men took a canoe and went out to meet it. The Mohawk chiefs and the old men made a treaty never to be any more fighting between the

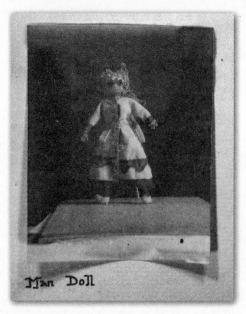

Man Doll

Mohawks and Milicetes. Every year some chiefs from each tribe came there to ratify the treaty. The last meeting was held thirty years ago. The Injuns called the place Mûn-kwād-ĭk, 'The Selling Place.'" (buying place, lit.)

The present Munquot or Munquart is probably the place referred to, for there is a short bend just above there.[22]

Milicete Bibliography
History of New Brunswick, Gesner, Indian translations

Edward Jack of Fredericton, in local papers from time to time

Geographical Reps, Gesner, Saint John, 1839, few geographical names

Explorations in Labrador, Hind, incidental references [added in red: "had Milicete canoe"]

"The Maiden's Sacrifice," *Saint John Sun*, about 1881 or 1882

In Divers Tones, [by Charles G.D.] Roberts, two legends, Moose and Gluskap

Algonkin Legends, N.E. Leland, Edward Jacks wrongly accredited to Micmac?

New Brunswick
It is commonly believed that the present New Brunswick was Sunbury County of Nova Scotia and the present New Brunswick and Nova Scotia comprise the Acadia of the French. But in *The Conquest of Canada* it is said that the French restricted Acadia to Nova Scotia and gave the name "Nouvelle Ecosse" to New Brunswick. [note added to journal in

red pencil: "New Scotland? Surely not"] The explanation perhaps is that the French occupied one part, the English the other, and that Nouvelle Ecosse (New Scotland) was a mere recognition of the English name, but they also gave the name Acadia to all that they claimed.

Indians' Personal Names

Ambrose Lockwood [in pencil: (Rookwood)]
Joe Alexander
Ned   ″
Francis Perley
Peter Joseph — Peter Joe — Pete Joe
Gabriel Joseph — Gabe Joe
John Solis
Joe Laporte
Jack   ″
Mitchel ″ Misel
Tom, Peter, Ambrose, Newell, Bear; ("Bar", Moo-in)
Newel or Noel Sapier (Sapiel, St. Pierre) nicknamed
   "Madewess" (porcupine)
Noel Paul
Noel Francis Sapier "Madewess" [in pencil: porcupine]
Sabattis (St. Baptiste)
Gabe Lolar

Injun Conversation

"You gonto have sometins heat? You want sometins heat?"
"Take care, you hapset."
"Looks like some kinds of rain mebbe."
"Just same one Ninjuns." (Just like an Indian)
"Spose mebbe you give me some flour. Take pity on squaw? I eat my last breakfast this mornin'."

"Little walk, much look-um." (hunting partridges)

"White mans make big fire git way off: Injun make little fire small fire git up close."

"Otter like injun, stop anywhere night comes; beaver like white man, he buildum house and clear land."

"Take pity on squaw, give me some flour, I eat my las' breakfas' this mornin'."

Indian Children

The Indian children amuse themselves in imitating the hunts of their elders. The boys make little bows of straight grained cedar and shoot the small birds around the camp. They grow very skillful and recount with great eagerness how they got *po-kwi-snau-i-es-sis* today or *Na-na-mik-tcis* (Spotted sandpiper) yesterday.

With spears made exactly like the big salmon spears, they wade in the brooks spearing suckers or small chubs along the river in schools.

They make a throwing stick, of a stick some three feet long, with the end flat and a piece of leather attached to that end and that again to a string, which they hold in their fingers letting go the string as they throw.

The Indian boy gets to be a good canoeman. At fourteen or under they can take their place as the bow poler in going upstream or tend the stern on salmon spearing trips of their elders.

They love to make toy bark canoes, but the workmanship is very crude. I have seen them in an eddy of the river with a flat piece of bark with stick the little canoes and a flat piece of bark set upright for a sail.

He whittles out a nice pole of cedar. Cedar whittles so well and is so stiff and light. And he wanders up and down the brooks and river near home. And when he brings back to the wigwam a nice string of trout, old Nokomis (grandmother) smiles and calls him I-so-ma-gwess-sis, the young fishhawk.

Indian children

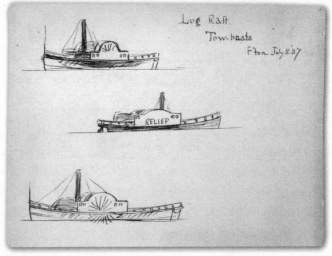

Log Raft.
Tow-baats
F'ton July 8 87

RELIEF

He is well acquainted with the names and looks of birds, fish, and animals and can imitate the songs of Atalagwauktum (hermit thrush), or Sulsulsili (savannah sparrow), or Moliskus (American widgeon).[23]

He gathers sweet hay and strawberries in season and later when chokecherries are ripe his lips get black and puckered. There are hazelnuts on the high ground that the striped squirrel has missed; flagroot in marshy spots by the river banks. There are groundhogs to be dug out of their holes in the bank by the help of Muin (black bear) or Skinosis (boy), his dog. And when snow comes he sets snares and catches rabbits.[24]

Old Margaret the Squaw

"You know Newell Paul [of] Woodstock. His son married one of my daughters. I write my daughter come up live with me and I give her house to live in. I got three houses and I give her one for nothing. But Newell Paul['s] son, he no like to come. He don't like leave old folks. Newell Paul he don't live at all. He cook outdoors in summer time and live in camp. I don't like have my daughter live that way. That's old time way. If you see Newell Paul, tell him you see me and tell him to write me a letter and let me know how he gittin long. We write letters up here, but that Newell Paul he never do write. I never know how he gittin long, since I been down Woodstock way last spring. That's no way, that's very poor way to live.

"When I come up here long time ago, oh mor'n thirty year ago, find plenty salmon out in the river. Plenty of everything and Injun don't have no trouble gittin something to eat.

"You go out in the river them times and ketch, oh mebbe seven or eight salmon in a little while. Now don't ketch one hardly.

"Seems like that government down Fredericton try let Injun starve. He make law can't ketch no salmon up here. He letum ketch the salmon when they fust come way downriver and they ketch most all

Humboldt Sharp, sitting

of them. And they get in the nets all the way comin upriver, and then mebbe no salmon git up here. Can't ketch him then, Injun ain't 'lowed ketch him there.

"I think that government better send soldiers up here and shoot all the Injuns. Good deal better do that than let Injun starve. Injun starve like it is. Better send soldiers and kill Injuns. Good deal better die that way. Then we die quick. Now we die slow."

Humboldt Sharp

September 24 Humboldt Sharp,[25] a young man of about my own age, got back from the west where he had been for above a year, a few days before. He got home by a morning train, was greeted by the family and the dog "Purps," ate his dinner in the afternoon, took his old gun down off its rack, and the two of us were out in the foundry woods[26] after the partridge. Purps had been so long without the restraining guidance of [his] old master that he saw nothing but squirrels and groundhogs, and the fine old drummer[27] [partridge] we had to find ourselves. Hum had been away a year and had not seen a member of his family. It shows how the woods spoil a man. Thereafter began a series of excursions into the woods, both long and short ones, that were of the greatest enjoyment to me, and I had in Hum one who could understand how I felt without a single word between us.

The following Sunday we were off again, shot partridges which we ate and caught a string of trout, and we built a little fire and broiled them on sharp sticks with salt and boiled a kettle of tea. Hum was an old hand in the woods. He had hunted bear and trapped quite a little.

"I tell you about the time when I was the worst scared:"

Humboldt's Adventure on "Roostic"

"I went up with ———— up onto the Ox Bow[28] in Maine. We went to Presque Isle and then we got a team to haul in from there. It was in the fall of the year and we had a barrel of flour and we stayed there six weeks. I shot a bear and one time I was going through the woods and I come on a caribou and I was that close. I had nothin' but my axe and I threw that at [it]. It come on to snow and we went out one morning to go round the traps when we come onto a fresh bear track made that very morning. I sees it was making for a lake that was two or three miles away and I thought he might be goin' there for he was keeping a pretty straight course. So I said to the fellow that was with me, 'Suppose you keep on the bear's track and I will take a short cut to the lake and maybe I can head him off.' So I started off and he kept on the track.

"I don't think he much cared to follow the track; he wasn't much used to the woods. He kept on and the bear had stopped some and warn't as far ahead as I thought. Well, the feller kept on and just as he come to the top of a little ridge and looked over, there was the bear a'smellin' under an old cedar. They weren't over two rod apart and the bear looked up and I don't know which was the scaredest, the bear or the feller. The feller, he turned and run, and the bear, he turned too.

Humboldt's friend
and the bear

"Well, I went on till I come out one side of the lake. I didn't see no tracks and I knew he hadn't got there. The feller agreed to meet me at the lake sure, so I went around to the other side and I found beaver works. I waited there and every little while I shot off my gun to let him know, if he was around. I stayed there till it come on to grow dark and still he didn't come, and I saw I would have to fix her up for the night. I picked out a place right alongside the lake under a big cedar where there

weren't much snow and when it
come on dark I had a big fire on
each side of me and I picked a
few boughs for a bed. There was
plenty of old dead wood and I
gathered a big lot of that. I laid
down between the two fires. I
had the nine-bore gun of Henry
Green's and I had that 'longside
of me. I went to sleep and it was
along in the night when, I didn't
know what it was, you know how

Humboldt and the owl

something wakes up and you wake up but you don't know what it is.

"I laid there wide awake lookin' up into the black limbs of the
cedar. Just then something give a scream right over my head and I
thought my time had come. I just laid there trembling.

"Then I sees two eyes like coals of fire right over my head. Injun
devil says I to myself. The sweat come out all over me. The fires was
all out. I sees there was just one thing but for a minute I could no
more move a hand than I could fly. Then I shuts my teeth, jumps to my
knees, gives the fire a kick. A little blaze flickers up and I sees what it
was. I drew a bead between the two eyes and fires. The thing come to
the ground with a dead thump. It was an owl.

"That made me mad about the feller not comin' when he said he
would, so I said to myself, I'll let him stew. I went over to the nearest
settlement and I stayed there two days and then I went back. The feller
told me about the bear. He was pretty near scared to death. He told
me he went to the camp and he had barricaded himself in and he hadn't
hardly dared to stick his head out the door all that time.

"That was the worst scare I ever got. I thought the Injun Devil had
me sure."

"Purps"

Dear old Purps, companion of many a hunting trip. Everybody's dog, nobody's dog. Not even could a name be agreed upon. He was simply the pup. From the pup it became "pups," from that to "purps." When I came on the scene, Purps was two years old, and from puppydom, with all its trials, he was developed into a large, smooth-haired, shapely dog of thirty or forty pounds, black and shiny, a tan muzzle, of uncertain ancestry, but suggesting more of the pointer and a touch of collie. A fine nose, and a natural hunter like all right dogs.

Purps's master was away in the west and he took me to himself a new master and we always went out together, I to carry the beloved gun, Purps to show where the squirrels and groundhogs were. After Hum got back we had a hard time breaking him of these bad habits but we soon made of him as fine a dog for partridges as there was in all Carleton County. The method of hunting partridges [for him] is different from what it is with us.

Purps chasing the groundhog

Purps sleeping

The business of the dog is to find and rout the birds, put them to a tree and sit down underneath until someone gets [there], all puffing and blowing after maybe a hard run of half a mile, while the dull bird sits there rigid as death with elated crest and dilated eye. A good rifle shot shoots the head off but those were not yet the days of rifle shooting and a charge of birdshot, not always in the head, nearly always brought the bird down where Purps felt he had the right to take a few mouthfuls of feathers out as his reward.

Purps would not hunt, either, with those who missed a bird two times in succession. Oh no, no excuses for him. He left such people and went home. They were usually people who "borrowed" him. He expected people who borrowed him to know their business. A man who borrows a dog should know his peculiarities.

The woodchucks were his greatest fun, and when he couldn't or didn't have a hunt on with the man pack, he went off on his own hook. He knew where the groundhogs were. They would be in holes in the sandy banks of the river and Purps would go there. It was astonishing how he could dig. The sand was not very solid. I have seen him go right in out of sight and nearly out of hearing, too.

One time he got after a groundhog in the bank by a field where men were putting in nursery stock and I guess the groundhog thought it was time to get away so he begun digging and Purps right after him. Pretty soon the men saw a groundhog's head pop up through the soil ten or more feet from the edge of the bank and then the whole hog and it started and took across the flat field. It was about two hundred yards to the edge of the woods.

The hog had not got half way there when up popped Purps and he wiggled out of the hole, looked around to see the way the hog had gone, and started. The hog had the start and before Purps could catch it, it had reached the woods, and when Purps got there it had found a crevice in the rocks and what the men saw was a much frightened groundhog crouched down in the crack and Purps, his nose only a few inches away, but utterly powerless to reach it. All the barking he could do didn't move the groundhog. When it came dinner time Purps gave it up as a bad job.

The Gibson Deadwaters — First Trip
September '87 Hum and I took the wagon and old John [a horse], Purps, ammunition, shotguns, grub for several days, went down six miles on the west side of the river to the house of some people that Hum was acquainted with and here we left the horse and wagon, and piling our stuff on our backs, took in on an old road called the Old Bull Road. [It was] once a well-cut, plain road on which timber had been hauled out to the river, but now it was all choked up, and cord wood had been hauled out from many places on both sides of the road. As there were much newer [tracks], it was [a] most difficult matter to follow the original road, which led onto the heart of the unclaimed forest.

We were to go only as far as the Four Mile Brook, then turn down it a short ways to the dam and deadwater of the Gibson Brook, a stream of considerable size, full of trout and a great resort for water birds as well as bears in great numbers, and caribou, mink, otter, lynxes, foxes, sable, black cat, but few moose and no deer, with undergrowth that [sic].

We had not gone far before we came to the end of the road which showed that we had unawares turned off the right one. Instead of retracing our steps we concluded to keep on. We tramped on and on. It grew late. We did not come to any stream like the Four Mile Brook and we were soon lost in a great spruce swamp. We struck a brook and thinking that was the right one, turned down it expecting to reach certain landmarks well known to Hum.

We were crossing an alder swale when I glanced up the top of a small birch tree and I saw what I thought was a bear cub. It nearly

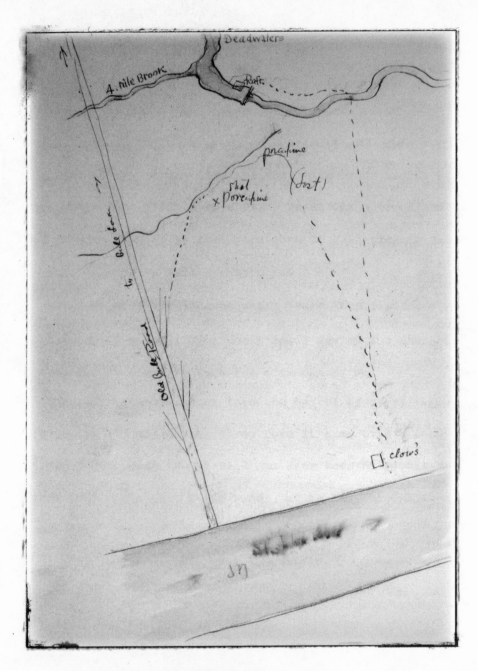

Map: Gibson Deadwaters area

scared the life out of me. I dropped some buckshot into the barrel of my shotgun and, aiming at the black body, fired. Down it came with a thump. [It] was a porcupine, the first I had ever seen. No sooner had I fired than Purps was on the scene, but he had once had an experience with them and he did not take hold.

Being the first, there was nothing I could do but skin it. The keen spines came loose and stuck into our hands, but we soon got the hide off and I folded it up the best I could and tied it and, suspending it in my belt, started proudly on. We shot some partridges and these I hung to my belt as well. We did not know where we were going. We met with lots of fresh bear sign and pretty soon we came upon another porcupine. Purps found it first and when I fired at the thing the dog, excited, ran upon the quarry and suddenly drew back with a nose full of spines sticking out like a pincushion. The dog began to whine and paw with all his might. Hum seized him and helped hold him down, and while Purps wriggled and cried, we drew out the quills that were rapidly disappearing. When we got to the last one, it had buried itself into the dog's nose, all but a quarter of an inch. That cured Purps of porcupines.

It was now dark and we discovered that we were lost. One thing only we could tell by and that was the glow of the set sun in the west and we knew that the settlement lay in that direction. There was nothing to do but go that way. The trials of that [day?] will never be realized. It was pitch dark and it seemed as if we must have crossed every bog, swamp and tangled blowdown in that whole woods.

The porcupine got undone, and every time it slapped against my leg two or three quills got into my meat. I had to stop to get these out and then flounder on awhile to get more into me. Humboldt led the way, whose location in the darkness I could only judge by the crashing of limbs and his execrations at the tangles he was getting into. Whenever the quills struck they went in a quarter of an inch. One slap and then if

Purps barking at the porcupine

they weren't pulled out at once they proceeded to crawl in the rest of the way, and after they once got a hard set were hard to pull out.

At last we struck a back pasture, then a house where lived a Scotch Presbyterian. The partridge were not fit to eat. It was not safe to try — they were literally filled with quills, and much to my sorrow I had to leave not only them but the hide. We stayed there that night. It was Sunday morning. We didn't like to tell such good people that we meant to find our way back by a fresh start, so we pretended we were going upriver and then struck back, found another road which took us in without trouble to a small the brook [sic] and thence up to the dam.

At the dam we found most of the water run out and the banks were bare, save for the dead standing trees on the shores at the edge of the green woods that grew [illegible]. At the dam, lying on the shore, we found a large raft and on it was a house of boards. It had been used as a cooking raft in [lumber] driving time. We found a stove inside. There were a number of great blue herons about and we heard ducks quacking. Hum and I went up the shore, he on one side, I on the other. Fresh tracks of caribou were all over the flat. While I was creeping up on a flock of black duck, Hum was having some fun. The dog was with him. He, too, was trying to stalk some duck, and the dog was crawling along on his belly behind him, when out from the woods stepped four caribou. Hum waited till they came within fifty yards and then let the leader have it.

The caribou fell then got up and before the dog could fasten hold he had started and gone to the woods, and then the dog had to give it up. I went up to the place.

We slept that night in the little house [on the raft]. In the night we were awakened by a splashing near the raft and getting up and peering out of a small window we saw nothing. We could hear, at apparently not thirty yards, some animal walking about on the beach and pawing the water. We did not know but that it might have been a bear. Finally

Kitchen on raft, Gibson Brook, Woodstock, September, 1887

we went out on the raft and listened but could not locate the sound. The caribou came in the night just across the stream while we looked out of the small window and then came out on the raft in hope of seeing what it was but we couldn't see the least thing in the darkness. It seemed at times not thirty feet off but in the darkness not a ripple could be seen. In the morning we found tracks of caribou where they had waded down right close to our camp. One could have thrown a brickbat to where they were.

We went back up to where Hum saw the caribou and while we were lying in wait for some ducks an adult white-headed eagle came and sat on a stub about sixty yards away. Intent on [the] ducks himself, he did not notice us. We could have shot him easily.

Then we went down below the dam and while there we heard a great to-do and then a flock of great blue herons came flying precipitately down the creek and at their heels was the eagle. When he got to where we were the eagle suddenly dropped forty feet straight, missed the heron which with a loud squawk smashed into the alders, and the eagle went on; but it was the prettiest strike I ever saw. We got lots of partridges that trip and went home contented.

I had by now given up the idea of going through college and so wrote to my mother. The Sharps persuaded me to stay after my sister had gone away and I was to do some tutoring for my keep. The northern winter crept on and ice formed in the still places of the stream.

Accident to my Foot
December 14 Hum and I took horse and sleigh, drove upriver several miles, then turned in on a road that led in towards Nackawick Settlement,[29] and we kept on this road until we came to a house at the edge of the woods. There, in care of a man named Gittis we left the sleigh and leading the horse took to a newly-cut lumber road. It was dark when we started in and we had a good deal of trouble keeping to the road. There was several inches of snow on the ground. After a walk of about two miles we came to a small clearing in the forest. Lights glimmered and we heard the tinkle of bells as the loggers were turning into camp. It was a lumber camp run by a man [also] named Gittis. He was the dirtiest big man in sock feet and black grizzled face and uncombed hair came to the door [sic]. A crowd of thinly clad children stuck their heads out and a couple of curs commenced to bark, but the big black man called them off. Inside there was not much room, but I have thought to myself many times since, people may be poor but they don't have to be poor and dirty both. We got permission

to leave some of our things there and then the road being pointed out to us we started into the woods.

Jud Hale (a brother of Fred Hale, the member of Parliament at Ottawa) was at the camp and gave us the usual welcome of the woods. This was [a] fishing trip. The deadwaters of the stream three miles away was the nearest water course and Hum said it was simply filled with trout which could now be caught through the ice.

We stayed that night in the lumber camp. After the manner of most camps there it consisted of one large room of peeled logs, with the berths, a long upper and a lower at one end, and at the other the cook stove and a space set aside for the cook. Along one side, in front of a window, was a long table with benches for the men to sit on. It was a large, comfortable camp, but the crew was not a large one, there being not over twenty-five men divided into choppers, swampers, sled tenders, cooks, teamsters, etc. There was another log building for the horses and oat bins, shop, etc. scattered around.

Next morning Hum and I went to the deadwaters and cut holes in the ice and fished but we only caught a few trout. It came on to snow. We built a bough shelter but we were so miserable that we finally went back to camp and next morning Hum took the horse and went home, leaving me. I meant to stay a week or two there as a boarder. The 16th, 17th, and 18th I spent about the camp, helping the cook whatever I could. The 17th was Sunday. Juddy [Hale] had gone away and some of the men had gone out to the settlement and when Monday came several had not returned. The evening before, John Ring, the acting boss, who had observed that [I] was a fairly good chopper, said, "Suppose the Yankee goes out to help us in the morning." I agreed to do so, rather liking the novelty and desirous of being obliging. The boss gave me an axe and a whetstone and before daylight I was up with the men. The axe was as sharp as a razor, and it had an extra long handle, presumably for long folks like me.

My crew of two or three choppers and teamsters went out a little ways and we pitched in. I was a swamper. The business of a swamper is to follow the chopper and when he had chopped down a tree to cut out a road to it so a team of horses can get in to it with a bobsled and make fast to the end and twitch it out to the yard where the logs are piled up in tiers on skids and later on they are hauled on double bobs five or six at a time to the landing where the water will carry them out to the main river where they are either rafted to some mill or floated down to the booms at Fredericton.

I was at work a few hours. I had shed my coat and was working in only a red flannel undershirt. My chopper had kept me working pretty lively and I was not used to the work. But I happened at length to catch up and in that case my duty would be, while he was limbing the log, to get upon the log and chop it off. This is done usually by standing on the log and making one cut to the middle then turning around and making the other cut.

The tree had fallen and instead of dropping prone the limbs held it about six feet from the ground. I mounted the trunk, marked out the spot where I was going to cut the log, chopped the small limbs away around that might catch the axe, and made the first cut to the heart. Then I turned in my tracks to make the other. I took out the first chip and had raised my axe for the third blow when a twig caught the blade, turning it, and with full force the blade of the axe went across my right foot.

I shouted to my chopper that I was cut. I think he lost his head. I got down off the log and held the two parts together, for the axe had gone through three pairs of socks and an arctic overshoe, nearly severing the foot at the great toe joint. The men came running from all sides. I tried to get someone to take my suspenders off to tie my foot up but it was some time before I could make anyone understand. They had completely lost their heads at the sight of the crimson spots on the snow. At length I got them to understand and I wrapped up my foot so that there was no escape of blood. That was about nine o'clock in the morning.

Supported by two men I limped to a bobsled. I was hauled to the camp. The next thing was the doctor. I did not realize the seriousness of the thing and I had some notion that being in perfect health as I was I could take care of the thing myself and in a few weeks would be around.

But they told me I must have a doctor. Juddy's man happened to be there by pure accident and he was going in [to town], otherwise I should not have gotten away so soon. We started in but I had to go as far as the clearing on a light sled and of all the tortures of that two mile bouncing and sliding about as the sled went over the roughest road I thought I had ever been on. There was no possibility of driving gently; it was no fault of the driver. At the settlement Juddy's man with a sled came for me. My foot all done up in a flour sack now began to pain fearfully, more I think from the confinement, for there was no bruise; the axe had done its work like a razor.

When I reached Woodstock the circumstance that was the particular reason for Hum and I going away prevented me accepting the invitation to stay at the Sharps', so I drove to Woodstock and went to Mrs. Samuel Baker's on King Street. I walked up the stairs and awaited the arrival of the doctor. Doctor Smith came and took me in hand. George Baker held my knee as I sat in a chair. The excruciating pain of those few minutes will never fade from memory. Three arteries were severed. The pain of the attempts to tie them was more than I could stand. As each paroxysm came I grit my teeth and surged on the rungs of the chair. Then everything disappeared from my eyes. I saw I would probably faint. I told the doctor I had better take an anesthetic. The arteries had got out of the doctor's control. Dr. Sprague was sent for. I was given chloroform and when I woke up the pain was over, the stitches had been taken and there was nothing more but to wait till they grew together.

Mrs. Baker was very kind and so was everyone who was around me. I rested easily for a while, but soon it began to throb. By a fortnight the pain was constant, symptoms of blood poisoning. The doctors took hold again. The trouble was removed, the healing began rapidly and in six weeks I was able to be about and soon was able to put on a loose moosehide moccasin.

About this time two or three of the men in the camp dropped in to see me. They had just got out of the woods. After some hesitancy one of them asked me if I had received any money. It was the first I had heard. Then they told me every man in the camp had contributed, the total amounting to not less than twenty dollars. The men subscribed to it and it was deducted from their pay when they were paid off.

I got after months and months of dunning the sum of five dollars out of the boss of that lumber camp in full payment, and I got it only after incessant dunning for I felt that if the money did not belong to the men it belonged to me, for they had been charged with it.

So soon as I could get about I purchased a canoe from Maj. Dibblee and spent much of my time about the river and I came soon to be a fairly good canoeman.

Visit to Stickney's Mill
February 27 Mr. Stickney urged me to come out to his camp at Nackawick and so George Baker and I went out on the train. My foot was not healed but we took snowshoes. From the mill we went up and revisited the camp where I got hurt. We went back to Stickney but they wouldn't let us sleep in the berth because we had slept in the Hales' camp which they said was lousy. Young Davy Caldwell, the son of the cook, joined us for a trip across the burnt land, a distance of about five miles, back of Sow Back.[30] It was my second try on snowshoes and I had a piece of sheepskin with the wool [covering] my toe. The trip as well as the rate of speed could have tried a veteran;

through alder swamps where the shoe had to go edgeways walking
from log to log over blowdowns with jumps of five or six feet at the
end. I was getting behind all the time but at last we struck a road
where I took off the wearisome shoes and we went a little ways
further and came to a lumber camp run by the Haydens of Woodstock
and were made welcome.

Myself at Nackawick

The cook and one man only were left packing up ready to go away. They had a funny story of a nigger who worked there and how he run onto a bear's den and the bear jumped up under his legs and nearly scared the nigger to death. We went back on top of the sled load by road to Mapleton and from there walked to the mill. On March 6 we went back to town.

April 14 Went out to visit Davy Caldwell two days. Heard the *kup kup kup* of the saw-whet owl for the first. Could easily imagine how a lost person might think it was the sound of a sawyer filing his saw.

The snow began to go off and the water to rise in the river and the Meduxnakik[31] at Woodstock. I used to carry my canoe through town to a point above the booms of the mills and paddle around in the bog and the overflowed flats where the muskrats were and the crows were beginning to build their nests.

"Black Ike" and the Bear

Black Ike was a negro who was working in the lumber woods for Haydens up on Guimac[32] one winter. Black Ike was a swamper, the only colored man in the whole crew. (Negroes are a rarity in the lumber woods; they don't seem to like working out in the winter time.)

Black Ike was a swamper and the snow was about a foot and a half deep. The chopper goes on ahead and picks out a tree, cuts it down, and the swamper follows him with a road wide enough for a team of horses to get in with a bobsled to twitch the log out. Ike's chopper had gone in and was at work on a big spruce not far from the camp itself and Black Ike was following him up with a road.

Just where the road should be was a great pile of limbs and underbrush that someone had thrown there and Ike waded in singing and swinging his axe right and left. When he reached the brush he dropped his axe and began tossing the brush out of the way. He had just pitched one limb and stepped forward for another when the snow

Sawmill above dam, Meduxniac. Woodstock, July 30, 1887.

parted between his legs and up came a big bear right up out of the snow. It scared the negro pretty nearly to death. He gave a whoop that could have been heard a mile and everybody came running, thinking he was killed. The bear was just as badly scared, made off as fast as he could travel and was out of sight long before the other men got there.

"Golly, what was that?" The negro had got himself up out of the snow all covered from head to foot and began knocking the snow off himself utterly bewildered. "Ike, you got into a bear's den," said one man in a red flannel shirt. "The devil come pretty near gittin you that time."

"Golly dat bear took a rise outen me. He jest natchelly histed me outen de snow!"

"School" at Slipp's Store

During this while I could not wear a shoe of any kind and there was little for me to do. A fortuitous circumstance enabled me a little later to pay off all I owed Mrs. Baker as well as the doctor's bill amounting to sixty-eight dollars.

Across the street from the coffee house was a grocery store kept by my friend Whit Slipp and it was but natural that I should spend some idle time there. Here gathered or lingered from time to time all the wits of the village, especially of evenings when they were done with their day's work, mill men, lawyers, countrymen, even the genial mayor of the town. They loved the vigorous discussions that take place around the stove of the country store and it is a homely wit that flows there when "school" was in. Whit himself had a sharp tongue, a ready flow of language, and he could take the thrusts as well as give them. A keen appreciation of a joke and his invective was something one would think about before incurring the chance of a roast.

As in every town, there was one man who was always up to some kind of trick, not always to his credit, especially if [he] thought he was doing something "smart." There was one story that would hardly fail to bring him to terms when he was carrying things too far, and this is the story as Whit told it:

Vanwart's Christmas Goose

"One day in the fall of the year when people were beginning to lay in their meat and turkeys for Christmas, a man came into town with a load of geese all plucked nice and ready to cook. The old man went out and pretended he wanted to buy and looked over the whole sled load and he got his eye on what he thought was about the finest goose in the whole lot.

"When the man goes into another store, Vanwart slips the goose into a bag and walks into my store and drops the bag down behind a flour barrel. I didn't know it was there till Johnny Stairs came to me and told me what he had found. I kind of suspected something.

"There happened to be a dead cat out in the yard that someone had just shot and it was all stiff and a pretty big cat. I takes the goose out of the bag and puts the cat in and drops it back behind the barrel. The old man does not come in himself that evening when he gets ready to go home but he sends in his man and he puts it under the seat and drove over to the house. When they get over to the house Vanwart says to the man, 'Hang the bag up in the loft of the carriage house and don't let anything get at it.'

"The old man chuckled over the fine trick he had done and he didn't buy any goose or turkey that year. When Christmas morning came he went out to the shed and found the dead cat in the bag. Oh, he was mad, and it was too late for him to get another. The fellers never let up on him until he paid the man for the goose."

What became of the goose, Whit?

Whit only smiles and looks wise. "I didn't buy a goose that year myself either."

Jerry and Whit

The boys had gathered around the stove in the village store.

"What's that the widow said to you that time downriver?" asks Whit, with a twinkle in his eye. Long Jerry turns red in the face and Whit turns to the assembled crowd, who are waiting for the fun to begin.

"Jerry was downriver at the widow's at Eel River, and as Jerry was leaving she says to him, 'My dear Mr. Bragdon, do come again; I do so love to see you, you look and talk so much like my dear son George what's in the Penitentiary.'"

Old Jerry takes his medicine like a man and bides his time. Whit says confidentially, "I tell you, when you run up against old Jerry you have struck a snag. He's about as keen as they make 'em." And Whit gives a little laugh as he pays the compliment, and adds, "Old Jerry don't take slack from no one."

Whit's Bear

Whit had a rifle of which he was properly very proud. It was a Winchester of the original model of 1866, taking sixteen short .44-calibre rim-fire cartridges, an old-fashioned weapon. But it was a remarkably good weapon and Whit had done some good shooting with it.

It had once belonged to an Indian chief in Montana and he had given no one knew exactly how many ponies for it. It was handsomely nickel plated and the Indian had made for it a buckskin case, finely worked with a solid mass of beads on one side. The aforesaid chief had committed some indiscretion that the miners thought needed their attention, perhaps killed some other miners, and they fell upon the encampment of the chief, killed him, and a fellow in Missoula who was a friend of Whit's sent him this gun.

One day someone ran into the store and cried out, "There's a bear over the river. He's down in the field half way down the hill."

Whit jumped for his gun, not thinking of any joke, got into a canoe, paddled across as fast as he could and started up the field. It was all in plain view of everybody and there were certainly some objects up the hillside that did look like black bears. Whit crept on until he was sure he saw the bear standing on his hind legs behind a fence about two hundred yards and taking aim he cut loose. The bear did not move and Whit fired into it a good part of his magazine in rapid succession when he realized that it was only an old burnt stump.

Whit went back and the crowd gave him the laugh. Now, whenever Whit gets to running on it too hard on old Jerry Bragdon, who put the job up, all Jerry has to say is "Well, Whit, how about that bear?"

Canoe Upsets in the Creek

"The two fellers Adney and Baker had been up the creek. It was high water and they runs their canoe up on the boom up there by Moore's Mill, and steps out on the log to lift the canoe over. You know how a boom it starts to roll and keeps a'turnin' until the chains fetch up. They steps out on the boom, one at each end, and lifts the canoe up and jest as they were lettin' it down on the other side the boom started a'rollin' and the fust thing I seen was the two fellers in the water and the canoe upside down.

"Baker paid no attention nor nothin' but just finned her for the jam of logs close over to the mill. But the long feller hung on to the canoe and turned it right side up and got it to the log and they got into it and came on down. But you orter seen them when [they went] in, I tell you, their hats floated right off. I was standin' right on the shore and the long feller when he comes up with that long neck of his stickin' up through the foam and sawdust, and it seemed a yard long, a'stickin' up, way up, and lookin' around as if he was at sea and was a'tryin' to git his bearins.

"Old man Moore sticks his head out of the mill window and he hollers out, 'What you doin' in there, takin' soundins? Ye didn't think the bed of the stream had changed, did ye?' I hollers out, 'Say, you aint got a match, have you?'

"And when the feller crawled out, he was that long I thought he would never get all out and Baker was a'helpin' him. Old Sally was a'comin down the road and heard the commotion and stopped. She is kinder shortsighted and she couldn't see plain. She says to me, 'What's that man doin' over there, fishin' out rails?'"[33]

(We saved our gun, both the paddles and a mess of fish that lay in the bottom of the canoe.)

Tripping Tow-line, to Mouth of Aroostook

I lived in my canoe all the summer and as soon as I got able to do something, I went to work at the Sharps' making boxes for plums at one cent apiece, and when I had the material I could make a dollar and a half or more a day, but material was not always ready.

One such dull time when I was going up to Upper Woodstock, shortly after leaving town I overtook two tow boats going upriver. I came near and one of the men aboard hailed and said, "Come aboard, we'll give you a tow," an invitation I was not slow to accept.

I found they were two tow boats belonging to the corporation that drives the logs down the river and that they were going back as far as the mouth of the Aroostook where the corporation, alias Mr. Giverson, resided. It was a flat scow about forty feet long and nine in width. In the rear was a house with a low flat roof and on this stood a rough weather-bronzed man in high driving boots who managed a long wide rudder standing on the roof with the sweep between his legs. Just in front of the house was a short mast to which was tied a few feet up a rope about a hundred feet long and at the end of that a team of horses. From about the middle of the tow rope was a smaller rope that connected with the top of the mast and by means of this rope the tow line is tripped over obstructions such as logs and rocks. The other boat ahead was similar to the one I was on.

Our scow was full of peaveys and hand spikes[34] and we had a string of bateaux behind to the number of a dozen. A ruddy faced chap, evidently the boss of the crew, said to me, "How far are you goin' up?" To which I replied by saying, "Only to the Upper Corner."

"I tell you what," said he. "We hired two damn Injuns at Woodstock to go up with us to trip tow line and they put their damn birchbark aboard and never turned up. We're short of men and if you'll go along we'll pay you a dollar and a quarter a day and four meals a day."

"Why certainly," said I, "I've got nothin' to do."

"You can come back in your canoe."

The bargain was made and at once I was assigned to my new duties. On glided the boat and the hoofs of the horses clattered on the stony beach. Whenever the sagging tow rope came to a log or rock all I had to do was to seize the tow rope in both hands and throw my whole weight on it. After a while I got very skillful so that I could clear the obstruction with a wavelike motion of the line. But sometimes I missed or there were too many. The rope caught instantly. I would have to spring into the usually shallow water, flounder ashore slipping

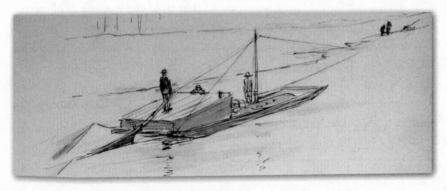

The towboat

and falling on the slimy rocks, and trip the line by hand and then get back on the best I could. The work wasn't so much fun after a while when the blisters began to come but there was no stopping when the line had to be tripped. And the moccasins were worse than rubber on the slippery rocks.

The man in the other boat fared worse than I did. He was a middle-aged person with a scraggy beard and seedy black "Sunday clothes" and he was trying to get upriver. Manual labor seemed out of his line and he had corns on his feet and when they got wet he was in awful trouble. He couldn't take his shoes off and he couldn't keep them on and his hands got all blistered worse than mine. But we made up for the hard work by the grub we got. The boss just laid himself out on that trip. It was the end of the hard driving season and they were going home.

"Boys," said he, "we might as well live as well as we can." We got up before it was light and ate breakfast. Then worked till ten and then had another full meal. Then we worked till about [sic] and had another and at dark or later we had the last and went to bed soon after. One meal was exactly like another. There were no finicky distinctions between breakfast and lunch. We didn't have to decide whether we would have oatmeal again or not, whether it would be a cold meat or a chop for luncheon. It was the same thing all the way through and it was the best the land afforded. Eggs, pork, bread and butter, the freshest, and strawberries and milk, and for luncheon it was the same. For dinner it was the same and the same for supper. All we could eat. It takes work and air to make a man hungry. We don't eat at all in the city. We mince and fuss and coax our jaded appetites and in the end die of indigestion.

July 19, 1888, Indian Village, Tobique
The men were very tired, for the last six weeks they had been working from daylight to dark, and that means pretty nearly eighteen hours in the summer time. And then to lie fifty to seventy-five men in one

long row under a tent with exactly eighteen inches of space for each man and you had to pull the long blanket up when your neighbors did. The steersman said he was going home and he was going to sleep right through for a solid week. And he looked as if he could.

We slept at nights in the cabin of the horse yacht[35] and we were three days and a half making the fifty-seven miles to the mouth of "Roostick." There we tied up the boats and carried all the stuff up and put it away and I steps up [and] gets a bill of my time and the four dollars and thirty-eight cents in good Canadian money and could then say that [I was] a fully fledged lumberman, having like every other good lumberman had a foot cut and worked on the drive, albeit the drive was going up instead of down with the logs.

Returning, stopped overnight at Francis Perley's at the Indian village on the Point at the mouth of Tobique. I slept between sheets in a house where there was an organ and a parlor lamp, things I had not yet learned to associate with Indians. Old Margaret was very talkative. (See notes of what she said.)[36]

Next morning I got a fairly early start. The wind blew very hard upriver and it soon began to rain. I took off my coat and vest, laid some blocks of wood in the canoe, and put the clothes on these and covered them with sheets of bark. To keep the bow headed downstream I had to pile rocks into the bow. I paddled harder than ever before, possessed by the utterly absurd idea that I must reach Woodstock in a day. In spite of the hardship I was making such good time that I bethought me to beat the night train down and so I worked with all the might in me. When the train crossed the bridge I was there but on the two miles to town the train got ahead of me. I was so exhausted that when I landed my canoe on the bank of the river I tried to lift it on my shoulders I made several [end of text]

A Trip in a Birch Canoe
Through the
SQUATOOK
LAKES
Sept. 24,
1888

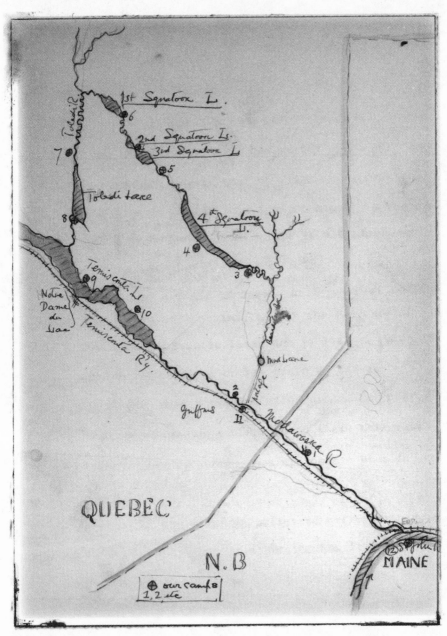

Adney's map of Squatec lakes area

THE SQUATOOK LAKES

One [day] Hum and I were studying over a large map of the Province of New Brunswick that we had pasted up on the rough wall of a room in the garret that we fixed up and where we molded our bullets and tanned our muskrat hides, a den exclusively our own where we could take refuge at all times and discuss our trips and plan for others.

"There's a chain of lakes," said Humboldt, pointing to a spot just north of the line, "and in the Province of Quebec it's called the Squatook Lakes[1] and I'd like to go up there.

"We could take a canoe up on the train as far as Little Falls, and it must [be] a hundred miles around the chain of lakes. I don't see why we couldn't go up there this fall. Nobody but a few Frenchmen ever goes up there. What do you say we go?"

It was never my policy to differ with Humboldt about matters like this. Even if I had thought it very wrong, far be it from me to lay anything in the way. There was from that moment, only [one] thing we could [do], and that was to make that trip to the Squatook Lakes without any delay. We thought of nothing else from that moment. We had a lot to do getting our outfit ready.

Hum bought some cotton and had the girls sew us up a tent, about six feet square,[2] open in front and when it was done we covered it with linseed oil and hung it on the line to dry. We bought an old birch canoe from the Indians and gave three dollars and a half for it with two paddles thrown in. It could not be said to be a very fine canoe but it was fairly good though very old. It leaked some.

We calculated to spend two or three weeks and this is what we got together: tent, heavy woolen quilt covered with sacking for protection, two sheepskins to lie on, an old hair trunk twenty-eight inches long, into the trunk homemade bread, biscuit, tea and sugar and salt, pepper and pork; one six-quart tin pail, tin dippers, tin plates, knives, forks, spoons, frying pan, fish hooks and lines; field glasses, axe, creel for ammunition, etc., waterproof canvas bag, plenty of rope to tie things in, a large dog named "Purps," two single-breech-loading shotguns, 10- and 12-gauge, warm clothes and moccasins. An imperfect outfit from many points of view but this was our first long canoe trip and we had no reason to expect the unusual conditions we met with.

We chose the time of year when mosquitoes and blackflies, those pests of the most beautiful country God has made [*sic*]. The nights would be cool and bracing. It was the most delightful time of the year in the woods.

It was the 24th of September when we put our canoe on a freight car and sent it off ahead of [us] and we followed on the one passenger train that runs up that far. It was night when we reached Edmundston and we went to the hotel of Felix Hebert pronounced Felix "a bear." We found our canoe had arrived and next morning early we took it off the train, put it on our shoulders and marched through the town above the mill and placed it gently in the waters of the Madawaska River and then we piled all our stuff in and arranged the canoe about as follows: Hum reserved the stern compartment for himself and his feet. In the next was the trunk and everything that could be got into that. In the third, myself with the tent for a seat, and in front the dog. We kept this order the whole trip.

We had a great deal of trouble with the logs that jammed in close to the mill. The river was filled with them. But after four miles we got clear of them and we had clear work. The river is so placid that we have hardly to use our poles. We met with our first mishap. We dropped the frying pan overboard in six feet of water. After about an hour's work we fished it out. We had to carry the canoe clear around the bridge of the Temiscouata R.R. that is just under way.

It is a pretty stream. It winds sluggishly through grassy meadows with here and there a clump of woods at the water's edge and there

View from our camping place mid[w]ay up the Madawaska

were little islands and bars and the water was so delightful and pure and cool. Sheldrakes[3] got up every now and then.

We pitched our tent not many miles up in an ideal spot, a low grassy spot in a clump of poplars and willows, and we built our first campfire of the driftwood on the beach. [See map on page 66 for location of camp one.]

On the following day it began to rain, a contingency for which we were prepared for in no way. We had no waterproof clothing whatever and we had to take it as it came and dry off afterwards as best we could.

Both of us worked paddling, and standing up and poling when we came to the quick places. It was a pouring rain when we arrived at the house of a man, Griffin, twenty-five miles from Little Falls. Griffin was the man who was to haul across to the first of the long chain of lakes. We went to his house and engaged him to haul us across the four-mile carry to Mud Lake. We had ideas of hospitality and we rather looked to Griffin to ask us to sleep on the floor of his kitchen or in his barn for it was continuing to rain harder and harder. We were thoroughly drenched and most miserable-looking objects. But no suggestion did he make, not what we would have done, we thought. We were young and we were proud and so with our heads as high as lords we went across the river to a thicket of white birches and there we pitched our tent and we built our fire and dried our clothes and spent as comfortable [a night] as one could want. [See map for location of camp two.] Everything is French up here and this is our first reception by a man presumably French or with a French wife. It did not give us a favorable impression of the French habitant of that part of Canada.

Next morning the rain gave us a respite. We carried Griffin half a mile down river in the canoe while his boy led a small, stunted, long-haired Madawaska pony down the other side and when we came to the place we swam the horse across.

Griffin proceeded to build a carry-all. He took two round spruce poles and laid on the ground two feet apart, the front ends being rounded off below and at each end, he pinned a cross piece, hollowed for the canoe to rest on, and boring hole with an augur and standards set up in the cross pieces. The canoe was laid on right-side up and we put all our things inside. The horse was hitched to the front and we made thus our long journey to Mud Lake. We ate some partridges we picked up on the way, bade our friend goodbye and started for the outlet of Mud Lake.

Guides are invariably taken whenever this trip is [made by a?] stranger but we started with no more knowledge of what was before us than we got from a map which located the lakes approximately but gave no idea of the character of the streams between the lakes. The wisdom of inquiring about these things was impressed on us before we were through.

We found the outlet of this mere pond, a lumberman's dam with a sluice through the water was rushing and pointing our bow for it, the canoe gave a shot and we were launched on the waters of the Beardsley Brook. Well for us that it had rained that night; well that someone had been through just ahead of us and had cut the obstructions out of the way. Who they were we had no idea but they were not far ahead of us.

It began to rain. The brook wound and wound and it seemed as if we would never get out of the woods. Making a sudden turn, we ran right onto three sheldrakes. They got up with great splashing. I reached for my gun but before I could fire the ducks were out of sight and the canoe crashed into a log at a right-angle turn. The tough birch stood that pretty well. The brook grew larger as small streams came into it and now we were out of the woods but we could see nothing but alders. The alders grew on both sides of the brook, leaned over till they interlocked and we were met by a wall. Had the water been lower we should have gone under the alders by simply dodging low. The current now was sluggish, the water deep. We were met by this wall of alders and our hearts fell. In the midst of a swamp of boundless extent, no ground in view that would afford a stick of wood to burn or a dry place to lie on, it was coming on dark. Sometimes we had to lift the boughs and pull ourselves under; now we had to go over; then we had to thread this thicket and there was no current to help us through and we could not reach bottom with our paddles to push.

The stream grew deeper and still it twisted but not interminably for we got clear of the alders and were borne out onto a large steady stream coming in from the right and full to the brink but still fringed with alders. The stream was now so wide it was clear paddling and we did paddle for all we was worth. Not a sign of dry land in sight and we were as if in a sea of swamp with no vegetation but the ever-present alder, which can grow in water, and now and then an elm.

Every little while we flushed the ducks and we drove them before us. We never got a shot but our eagerness to get a shot gave an impulse that put us farther on our way than our broken spirits would. I have never seen any stream that wound and twisted more than the Squatook River. It would not possible [*sic*] without crossing sometimes. At length a hill appeared in the distance but that hill successively went to every part of the compass, now in front, now behind. We seemed never to get any closer. Darkness came on, still we kept on.

After half an hour's work a dark bank loomed up with trees on it. We knew that was solid ground so without stopping to consider further we put our canoe in, crawled out on some cedars, for we could not get near the bank, and carried our stuff up a steep bank until we found a place level enough for the tent. [See map for location of camp three.]

The rain still came down. Hum got a piece of dry cedar out of a standing stub and we got a fire and our tent set up and will you believe it, we dried our wet clothes and slept that night as dry as a bone. There was nothing to be heard but the popping of burning wood, the dripping of the rain, and the snoring of Purps as he lay curled up between Hum and me. Purps always took the middle of the bed and as he curled up round instead of lying straight like a Christian he took up a great deal more space than he had a right to. But he generally had his own way.

We heard the tremulous mocking cry of loon and we knew a lake was not far away. In the morning we heard the sound of chopping and somebody must have heard ours for soon we saw a long black dugout with two men in it. They came near and they seemed to be Frenchmen and an ill-favored pair. From their sullen looks they evidently did not know what we were there for and after we had exchanged scant words of greeting they went away. We soon followed them and found that we had stopped within half a mile of good camping ground of the big (called the last) Squatook Lake.

The two Frenchmen were encamped at the head of the lake in a wretched shanty. We went ashore to make inquiries about the lake and the river below but met with such a cold reception that I kept an eye on my gun and we got out away from the most uncivil pair of men we had ever seen. We noticed a beaver skin stretched on a hoop hanging on the camp and guessed they were trappers and were inclined to be suspicious of anyone like us hunting there. They were a dirty lot.

We paddled a ways down the lake and made shore at a beautiful sandy beach in a deep cove to repair the broken bow of the canoe where we had smashed into the log.

This lake is fifteen miles long and not more than two or three in width and from its gravelly shores rose gradually high wooded hills covered with a growth of maples and birches turning yellow and with splashes of white spruce. We tried for trout, fishing out of the canoe where the headlands came down bold and rocky and we got some bites but we had no tackle that would hold them. We fished only bait and short line. Had we known how to fish with flies, what sport we would have had. They rose all around us in the quiet water as the evening came on.

We went a few miles on down the lake and went into camp on the left-hand side. It was a lovely spot underneath some old spruce trees, apparently an old camping place. [See map for location of camp four.]

Next morning, started for the outlet, we ran into a snow squall of some violence so that we had to seek shelter under the lee of a dale until it passed over. At the outlet were the remains of some whitefish weirs. There were great schools of chub on the sandy bottom a foot long. From the waters of the lake we passed into the quick current of the thoroughfare and now our real troubles began. These lakes, like all in this part of the world, are in course of change. Their beds gouged out by glacial action in the first place, the depressions filled with water on the melting of the ice, and as their levels continued to rise with rains they found outlets at the lowest point and have ever since been gradually cutting down their channels. As the land wore away above, the sediment gathered about the heads of the lakes and the present streams wind sluggishly in and out through the mud flats that they have deposited, and these flats are covered only with a growth of alder and a few American elms. At the outlet, however, where the cutting is still going on, the solid rock is laid bare and the water plunges and dashes. Then there may be a bit of stiller waters and it plunges and dashes again down, down, down. Many a time our hearts rose in our throats as we rose on our feet seeking vainly for a place to run in safety.

We knew nothing of this, nor how far it went more than the rough map showed. Our canoe leaked in a hundred places and time and again it seemed as if we would be dashed to pieces. Had we known where to go and which channel of the river to take it might have been different, but we had to let her go and simply take what came, down, down, down, like a never-ending stairway.

As darkness approached after we had gone we knew not how many miles, we camped near some enormous cedars and saw that our canoe would never stand much more. [See map for location of camp five.] So next morning we felled some straight cedars and split out some thin strips of wood which we whittled thin and lashed to the bottom of the canoe.

This is called shoeing the canoe. A canoe with shoes does not paddle well but it saves the bottom whenever it strikes a rock or when it is necessary to drag over bars. We ought to have thought of them from the start.[4]

We got our stuff in again and it was after noon when we got

started. We came to [a] jam of logs which we had to carry around and before we had been afloat half an hour the river began to wind sluggishly, as it does at the heads of lakes, and to our surprise we found ourselves at the head of the third Squatook Lake.

The third of the Squatook Lakes is only six or seven miles long and is surrounded by tall hills which instead of being covered with green woods are bare and bald from fires that seem to have destroyed many thousands of acres of land. Young birches and poplars were springing up but the beauty of the primeval forest was gone. There was a flock of white-winged scoters[5] here and when we came near they took wing and long as we stayed on the lake they flew up and down in single file at the speed of a railway train about three feet from the water. We gave them a charge of buckshot, but it fell far behind.

From the foot of lake number three we struck a narrow winding stream with much bulrushes and went into camp near the head of lake number two. [See map for location of camp six.] We got out lines, casting among the rushes and lily pads and caught an eighteen-inch chub. The meat was not fine but tasteless and coarse but we got no trout. Next morning when ready to start, Purps was not to be seen and presently we heard his strong bark up the lake and we knew he had something treed.

We paddled up partway and had an example of the wonderful echoes of these lake lands. The dog was barking on the right and it seemed as if there was a whole pack of dogs or wolves on the other side. It was uncanny and creepy. When we got to the barking, he had them all right. It was a flock of partridges and we got six. We thought we might as well leave the shoes off here.

Number three lake was three miles long and after passing through a somewhat wider river grown up with bulrushes came to the first of the Squatook Lakes. We amused ourselves trying to shoot a pair of loons here, and the loons in turn amused themselves by showing how they get under water before a barrage of buckshot reached them at point blank range. We had to give it up. The first of the Squatooks was hardly more than a pond and we were soon paddling down the easy current and soon a swift little stream came in from the northward on our right. It was Eagle River. The character of the stream remained slow and winding smoothly between banks as high as one's head with alders, elms, and ash trees and cranberry bushes.

We hoped to reach Toledi Lake[6] before dark but as we [went] leisurely along we were attracted by a path up the bank on the right and stopped. The path led up the level bank and there was the tiniest camp I ever saw, newly made, a little shed about five feet deep and about four feet wide, of sticks set up and covered with slabs of birchbark and with spruce boughs. Inside was a smooth bed of fir twigs and various small packages were tucked away where it was dry. The fire was only three feet away from the camp and consisted of ash logs set on top of one another with stakes behind to hold them in place.

We had some experience with Frenchmen and we did not know how it would be about stopping but we saw that not more than one man at a time ever lived in that camp and a small one at that. So we pitched our tent nearby. [See map for location of camp seven.]

We heard something fluttering on the opposite bank and going over in the canoe we saw a flock of partridges in a bunch of chokecherries. They let us come till we could almost touch them with our guns and we simply blew the heads off six, which were sadly needed. The partridge stews we made those days, there was never anything like them. We filled our six-quart pail filled it [sic] with water, put in two or three birds and a generous piece of pork (it hasn't the flavor without pork) and when it was nearly done we dropped in several large, round, hardtack biscuits as big as saucers and then plenty of pepper and a little sage. There was never anything left over from those feasts.

Our mysterious camper did not return and next morning we

started on, went a little way, came to more bulrushes and the head of a long lake. Here were lines set for cusk, a fish peculiar to those waters. We saw the head of a cusk back at the camp. Toledi Lake, for such it was, stretched away for twelve miles in a triangular shape.

We started for the outlet, or what we thought was the same. When we got there we found we had gone to the wrong corner and had to go back quite a way. We lost so much time we went into camp at the outlet. [See map for location of camp eight.] Beside we could hear the roar of rushing waters and we were on the lookout for the falls of the Toledi which were down off the map and were supposed to be dangerous. It was beginning to rain again.

Piling the stuff on the bank and covering it with the tent, we worked in the rain, cleared a place for the tent, cut the night wood, set up the tent, got a partridge stew inside, dried off, and lay down to sleep the sleep of the just. We could hear the dull roar of the rapids and we did not like it.

We got an early start, also three early partridges. The stream was rapid, broad, and shallow, rocks sticking out everywhere, so we had to go ashore and tie on the cedar shoes which fortunately had not been thrown away, and that was all that saved the canoe. She struck and scraped over rock after rock. We did not know the stream and there was simply no chance. We simply had to let her go and after a few thousand yards we had to get out and little by little let the canoe down over ledges of rock. In one place there was a drop of ten feet and we had to let the canoe down over there with utmost care. It was lively and a slip would have thrown us and the whole outfit would have been lost. It was the worst rapid we had come to yet. We kept a sharp lookout for the falls so as to carry around it.

The river got better for a while and we were surprised by the smooth sailing. Where we went ashore to lunch we got six more partridges. It seemed as if we had only to stop and the dog would put up partridges. We have never seen the like before or since. It was a beautiful winding stream with islands here and there and sandy bars. After traveling five or six miles and passing several minor falls or pitches we saw signs of civilization. Presently there loomed up on the right bank a large tent much toned by exposure, and landing we found it occupied by two genial young fellows and an old fellow, a smallish man with a bushy beard.

"How far is it to the Falls?" we asked.

"The Falls? You've passed the Falls. Didn't you see where they carried around?" We had, but that place did not seem so very much worse than what we had had fifteen miles or so after leaving the big lake.

"Did you see my camp?" said the old fellow. "That was my camp. I am going up there with another canoe load of traps and stuff."

They spoke English pretty well and they gave us a different reception from those we had [encountered before?]. The two youngish men were tending a whitefish weir that stretched across the mouth of Toledi, for this was the great Temiscouata Lake we saw before us. The old man brought out a letter for us to read. It was from a member of his family and he had had it I don't know how long waiting for someone to come along who could read it. The old fellow surprised us by telling us that he knew the Toledi so well he could come down it and never touch a rock, standing in the stern and snubbing with a pole.

When we came to leave one of the men walked out on the weir and took out a dozen whitefish and a trout eighteen or twenty inches long and of course we could only show our gratitude by presenting him with some partridges.

We were soon on the bosom of Temiscouata Lake (pronounced "Tomsquatta") stretching fourteen miles in each direction. Across, several miles away, we could just make out the white church and little cottages of the village of Notre Dame du Lac. We turned down the

Campsite nine, on Temiscouata Lake

lake and a squall broke upon us from the north, driving us before it. It was chilling and our hands grew stiff holding the paddles. We tried to rig a trysail with the tent but nearly swamped and gave it up. We drove before the storm for several miles until we were opposite the village and then, unable to turn broadside to the waves, got in the shelter of a rocky promontory and made camp where some stunted trees kept off the wind. [See map for location of camp nine.] All during the night the gale continued and the waves pounded off the rocks as I have seen only at the sea.

The wind was down the lake and against the rocky capes the waves dashed with fury. In the morning the wind had gone down but the seas were still running high. We ate the last of our fish and were entirely out of bread. We had to do something. It was a dangerous — nay foolhardy — thing to attempt but we had either to wait there hungry or get across to the village. It was like launching a lifeboat through the surf. The waves run so high that again and again we were tossed back. At length, wading far out, we got aboard and headed her into the teeth of the waves.

Our canoe was eighteen feet all over and thirty inches wide, loaded dangerously near the gunwales. Heading into the waves would not take us across. To turn across was to instantly swamp. We headed therefore, quartering, but even then water came over the sides, and when we got endways I have seen the thin bows of the bark dip and the water pour over both ends. Hum was kept bailing, paddling hard a while till the water got too bad, then bailing again, and we kept up this, paddling just as hard as we could, for two miles when we got under a lee shore and made the village.

The first thing we did was to strike for a store. We went up the steps into a small store where a little of everything was kept, from a side of bacon to a sheet of writing paper or a piece of bed ticking or a fishing line. The storekeeper was French. Everything is French up here and there [is] not English understood except by traders and those who have been to work in the lumber camps. Neither Hum nor I knew enough French to be understood and we had to make our wants known by pointing and by signs. At length we got some groceries and then inquired for the baker's — *boulangerie* — we knew that much French.

"Have you bread?"

"Bread, bread, no compron, Oh yes, yes, pain pain oui, oui, boulanger, one mile," pointing down the lake. "Pain one mile."

We thanked him and bought a square yard of cloth for a sail. Then boiled the kettle on the beach and then paddled what we thought was a mile down the beach lake.

I tended the canoe while Hum went after *Boulanger*. I waited and I think it must have been an hour when Hum got back with an arm full of bread.

"Where do you suppose that baker's was? Why, I had to go back all the way. It was only a little way from the other store. One mile. I suppose a Frenchman thinks that was a mile." Hum hadn't a very good opinion of the ordinary Madawaska Frenchman. Raise a little buckwheat and then do nothing but fiddle and dance all winter.

We laughed a good deal about the Frenchman's "mile" but there was a mile we did not know about; that is, the Tobique Mile and they calculate it by starting a good healthy caribou and then running him to death. As no one has been known ever to run a caribou to death, the "Tobique Mile" must ever remain an unknown quantity.

Rigging up our sail, we scudded before the breeze but finding the distance to the outlet too great, put into shore and camped in a grove of slender birches and poplars. [See map for location of camp ten.]

I do not remember whether it rained today or not but we got our six partridges again, two of which were drumming.

The next day took us to the outlet where the big trout are found. The member to Ottawa[7] got twenty-two trout, weighing forty-eight pounds that year.

Ten miles further on through, with frequent clearings and the little houses of the French settlements, brought us again to Griffins. Griffin proved not to be French but Irish, had married a French woman and had half a dozen or more children, who preferred French to English. I think we left him some partridges and gave him his augur, which he had left at the carry and which we had carried all the whole eighty miles.

We had a week of much rain and hardship but lots of excitement and were anxious to get down the one hundred and forty miles of river that lay between us and home. The water was high in the Madawaska and we made the voyage to Little Falls in short order. There we had a high mill dam to go around. It was noon when we arrived.

The dam was an apron dam with one slope of forty degrees, then it turns to about twenty and with a clear leap of four feet it was a drop shoot and a swash, then it left in a series of waves and masses of foam. On each side were eddies and there was a jam of logs in the right bank eddy. We looked at the dam and we says to ourselves, "We haven't stopped for anything yet — we ought not to stop for this."

We interviewed the mill man.

"Oh yes, small boats often went over." He lied. They never dared to go over and every bateaux expected to take in water.

"Suppose we try it," says Hum.

"All right," says I.

As a precaution, we took our stuff out of the canoe and carried it around. Then we got into the canoe. It may be well to explain that instead of trimming level I knelt in the compartment next to Hum so that the bow was high out of water, for we expected that to go under.

We went several rods up, to get a long start, and when we were ready Hum and I called "Go!" simultaneously. Every man in the mill was at the window.

Our paddles struck the water and the canoe shot ahead. Our hope is to get over quick. We are ten feet from the brink — my paddle snaps. "Go ahead!" shout I.

We strike the pitch. The canoe upends and quick as a flash we drop like a toboggan and the water foams about our ears. The bow has gone under and the canoe is filling with water. Luckily, we struck the edge of the fall. A few strokes of Hum's paddle and my stick and we are almost in the eddy when we are borne against the logs and have just time to step ashore when the canoe goes under. We can see it between the logs. We are both wringing wet and we think our canoe is gone.

We fish around with poles and finally are able to work the canoe into the eddy and out clear of the logs. Then we haul it out of the logs, empty out the water, and I says to myself, I don't mean to be stumped with all those men there laughing at us. I'll show them something.

We still had to go around the logs. I stepped into the empty canoe and standing erect I put the canoe out into the rapids and the canoe dancing under my feet, a trick I had learned, and I brought it around

Over Little Falls

below the logs to a bit of beach where we drew the canoe out and found it twisted all ways. Every seam was open and we had to go to the village and get a lot of tallow and rosin and linen cloth, and with the hot rosin pitch pasted up every seam and crack.

When we got that done we started again and when I since looked at the Little Falls falls itself I shuddered as I looked and saw the rock in the center that we touched as we went over and then were carried into the broad surface of the Saint John. It rained that night and we camped beside some man's stack of driftwood. [See map for location of camp eleven.]

Next day it rained hard. We paddled all day and slept at a farmhouse on the State of Maine side of the river. [See map for location of camp twelve.] Our only apprehension was the Grand Falls and we were in doubt whether to go over that or not. It was only eighty feet of a fall.[8] We didn't like to go around anything now. But as we drew near we thought better and carried the canoe on our shoulders the mile or more through the village and below the gorge. The river had never been known to be so high in the fall of the year. It was within two feet of spring level and that same year Tobique was never known to be so high before or since.

Below the falls we came to a landslide and there was a train stalled and people out on the tracks in Sunday clothes. They waved to us as we dashed by. We raised our hats and asked if they had any word to send to Woodstock.

We stopped overnight at a farmhouse and when we got up, the river was full of logs and we learned that Connors's drive of two million feet of lumber had gone out of the Grand Falls where it was hung up from the spring freshet.

It was still eighty miles to Woodstock, nothing for one day at this pitch of water. Here and there a bank gives away and trees topple

Tobique Narrows

The well-worn canoe

into the water. We pass the mouth of Aroostook on the right, Tobique
on the left, the water roiling as never before in the narrows, so as to
be seen from the main river. On we go, helping the current by the
rhythmic pull of the paddles. We are strong as oxen and the steady
paddling is nothing. We reach the Bumfrau.[9] A party on the shore hails
us. We go in and there are two Scotsmen and four others in Sunday
clothes. They explained that they were bound on an excursion to Saint
John, had gotten across but trains were all washed out, the ferries
were all down north of Florenceville bridge, and they wanted to get
over. The two Scotsmen did not dare take their pirogue out. Would we
do so? Certainly, with pleasure.

So we unloaded and let two get in first. I guess they had never been
in a canoe and they were scared to death but we had them lie still and
then we started. I never paddled but once like that and that was in

the race when the *Pocahontas* was beaten by the *Black Diamond*.[10] Hum was masterful, the broad river rushing like a mill race full of logs and uprooted trees. After the most desperate work we gained the other side and found that we had not lost much.

They insisted on paying so we told them a quarter was about right and went back of course easier. When we touched [shore] we heard a dismal howl and saw on the other side poor Purps. He had swum over and he immediately plunged in again. He was carried way down river and it was quite a while before he got back.

We took the next two over the same way but the effort was so terrific that we reluctantly charged them half a dollar, making seventy-five cents for the whole crowd. We never knew whether that figure really satisfied them but we thought that figure about right.

The rest of the journey was uneventful. When we reached Hardscrabble [Upper Woodstock] we landed and turned the canoe and were thankful for the darkness that concealed two wet, bedraggled, and dirty specimens of humanity that stole away to their room.

An old, much battered canoe was found on the river bank next morning by a villager and he tried to sell it for two dollars, thinking the flood had left it there. We saw him in time to explain; he had failed to sell the canoe at any price. I finally persuaded him to take the canoe himself for the sum of one dollar and fifty cents. He himself has several fine canoes and he really is too good-natured and really needed a lending canoe. That was without the paddles.

Caribou Hunt to

AYERS LAKE

with Peter Joe and Hum Sharp

Christmas

1888

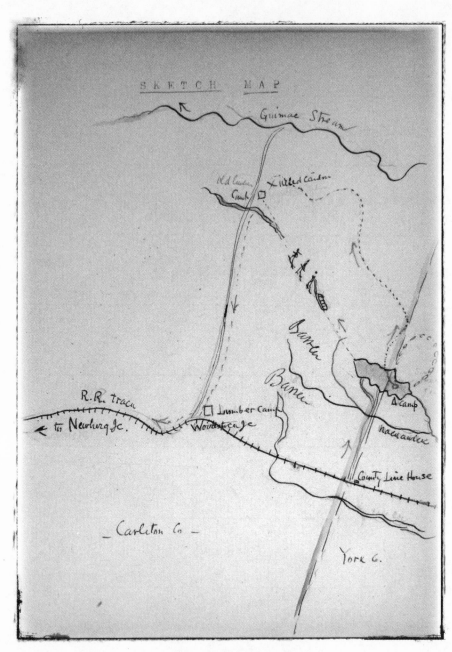

Caribou hunt to Ayers Lake

PETER JOE'S CHRISTMAS CARIBOU AND MY FIRST

One day in the early part of the winter, after the snow had come, Peter Joe said to me one day:

"I think I'll go kill um caribou, mebbe 'bout Christmas time, and git some wild meat for Christmas. Mebbe you like to go long? We kin take toboggan, some pork, some tea and camp out. Wild meat very healthy. Mebbe Gabe he kin go long, three be just enough."

"Where shall we go, Peter?"

"Oh, you know where that lake — what you call um Ayers Lake. I hear plenty caribou round there."

I was always ready for a trip of this kind. Gabe couldn't go but I didn't have to mention it twice to Humboldt.

Ayers Lake as it had been described to me was a small lake on the headwaters of the Nackawick. It was not over half a mile in total length and nestled at the foot of Sow Back Mountain at a high elevation, so much so that those who occasionally went there to fish it was a source of wonder they had to climb to the top of the hill to get to. On the side away from Sow Back the bank was low and was a nearly continuous descent for two miles to the railroad track. For better location, the county line between York and Carleton ran exactly through the middle of it.

The water was very deep. No one had ever got bottom and the trout ran to two feet in length but seldom would bite. It was a great country for caribou around there for there was much boggy and barren land and plenty for feed. The trains often ran into herds of them crossing the track and so, existing so near to civilization and surrounded by settlements not more than five or six miles distant in any direction, they grew to be wary beyond belief and came to increase greatly.

A few days before Christmas we took [a] train with all our traps and got off at the county line. There we packed onto the toboggan

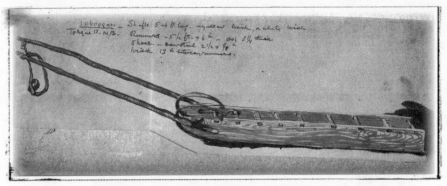

Tobóggan, Tobique R., N.B. (Peabody Essex Museum Neg. No. 32078)

blankets, a couple of flour sacks full of pork, biscuit, salt, pepper, sugar, and tea — Indians are inveterate tea drinkers — and an axe, a frying pan, [and a] tin kettle. All this was tied on with a rope wound over and over and the guns were tucked in last, and then getting into the snowshoes we started for the lake taking turns at the rope.

The Indian toboggan is a narrow sled fourteen inches wide, the runners being of cedar an inch thick and five feet long. Every eight inches are cross bars of hardwood. The runners are shod with a strip of beech wood two inches wide and bent up in front and back, the ends being tied down to the first cross bar with a thong of rawhide.

There was an old road we could follow. We saw old caribou track and got to the edge of the lake. When it was pitch dark we found a bark camp Peter had spoken about. It was by the edge of the lake, which was frozen over, and some trees had been blown across the camp. We got those out of the way, pitched boughs for a bed, built a big fire in front. Here was a lesson in camp building. It was a summer camp, being a ridge pole laid on top two crotches and poles were laid slantingly and [on] which sheets of spruce bark were laid. Somebody had peeled the bark of the trees near the camp and these dying had of course, when a wind came, fallen onto the camp. It was so cold that night that the limbs cracked open with a pop like a pistol.

In the morning none were frozen to death. Peter Joe, the only one who had hunted caribou, took command. We trusted the old Indian implicitly.

"I never go yet but I git caribou. My mother say I'm very lucky boy," said he as we threw our snowshoes over our backs and started across the hard surface of the lake. Here the lake was two or three hundred yards wide across. The banks wooded rose steep and beyond rose Sow Back.

"I guess best chance go back Sow Back, find caribou Guimac waters."

We set off up the mountain. I was not used to such rough work snowshoeing and I was stumbling and slipping. It amused the Indian when I fell down. "Sartain, fall down, very poor hunter." That moment Peter caught the toe of his snowshoe and buried himself in the snow and when he struggled to his feet he was covered with snow and the case only saved his gun. The muzzle of mine was full. We chafed Ambrose [sic][1] and said "Fall down very poor hunter."

We soon had to leave off our mittens and wished we had left our coats at the camp. We crossed over the ridge of the mountain then down the other side. Peter showed us what he said was a bear den under a big tilted tree and the snow was melted there. Why he did not rout him out I never understood.

Soon we saw fresh tracks in the snow, a band of caribou. Their track was a good deal like that of a cow. The snow was about a foot deep. They were wandering about nipping off tips of ground hemlock or yew that stuck up out of the snow. Peter felt of the tracks, found them frozen hard and said, "Bin 'bout two or three hours."

We hurried on and the tracks became fresher. Peter moistened his finger with his tongue and held it aloft. "Very bad, wind goin' toward caribou."

We witnessed the Indian's woodcraft. We did not follow the track but made detours coming back to it every few hundred yards. The tracks grew softer and momentarily we expected to run onto them. I carried the only rifle, a 57-calibre Snider-Enfield carbine. The Indian and Hum each had a single-barreled shotgun with round bullets. We followed the tracks and to our surprise they came out at the lake opposite our camp. We discerned tracks across the lake and ran across and found that the caribou had lately been right by our camp. Just where they were we couldn't tell. We went out onto the ice and were looking up and down the lake.

"I wonder what those men are doing up there," I said, pointing far down the lake. The Indian gave a single look. "Caribou." Now was indescribable excitement. My heart began to thump and pound. It was the first big game I had ever seen. There were two of them and they appeared to be coming our way. End-on, they had looked to me like men.

"One big one, one small one," said Peter. I had the rifle. "You git behind that bush," said the Indian, motioning to a thick fir bush at the edge of the lake.

"No, Peter, you take the rifle. You take it, Hum." I was so excited and I wanted the caribou more than the shooting of it.

"No, you take the gun."

So, long before they were in range I crouched down behind the bush, broke away the twigs that were in my range of vision. I took my hat off and laid it down and put all the cartridges I had in it, only a dozen. We did not know how they were coming. We supposed they would come, of course, to this side. But to our dismay they kept the other bank and came leisurely along, their heads swinging like a large colt's. There was one large one and a smaller one behind it. With rifle cocked, I waited. I had the place picked out where I should fire. They drew nearer and my hand trembled like a poplar leaf.

"Take the big one. I'll take the little one," said Hum. When they came abreast I covered with the big square sight and pulled and simultaneously rang out the report of Humboldt's gun. The caribou stopped with a jerk and I saw the snow fly up at the caribou's feet. The caribou stood smelling the ice where the bullet had struck and I fired again. Again, it fell low. Raising the muzzle, I fired again. Still, the caribou stood, not knowing where the shots came from. Hum had not touched his. Aiming for the fifth shot, I lifted the muzzle high. The animal's head was down, the wind was blowing strong down the lake. The shot rang out. The caribou wilted like a rag.

"Try the other," shouted Hum and I fired at the little one. "I've got two bullets in." When the big fellow fell the other ran to it and smelled. Presently the falled caribou raises its head. I wanted to go across and make sure of the one I had killed. "No, he's dead," said Peter. "Try little one."

The big one now rose to its feet, tried to step, stumbled and fell. "Try git little one," said the Indian. Again the big one got up, walked a few steps, stood stupidly, then staggered a few steps further and hardly before we realized it had got behind a jutting point. "He's all right," they said. My ammunition was all gone. The little caribou runs to the foot of the lake and goes into the woods limping from a wild shot of Hum's.

I started to run across to where the big fellow was when I hear a shout. "Lie down." I fall on my face on the ice and I see a caribou coming towards me. Then it swerves and crosses the foot of the lake. I notice for the first time that the Indian has not fired. But now he jerks off the cover and, as the caribou runs past at only forty yards, opens fire and Hum follows. I saw the balls strike the bank a few inches high and with a parting shot from Hum it gets into the woods without a touch.

We all now run over to where the big one was gone round the point, see a track in the snow. The track leads up the bank. We follow hot after. The trail goes over a log. "Pretty good for a dead caribou," thought I. The Indian is the better snowshoer and he goes ahead and I can only follow his track. I ran for about two miles and found the

Indian standing and alongside him were the fresh tracks of the band. There was a look of the greatest disappointment on the Indian's face. "Sartain, I thought him good as dead. Very big one." But somehow he had regained the band and they were now going down the hill twelve feet at a jump.

It was a sad disappointment. It was nearly night and there was nothing for us to do but go back. Hum thought we could get the caribou he had wounded. How we had hit the big fellow was a great mystery. "I see where he fall, where he fall a'gin two three times. I never think he git up off the lake."

We talked over what to do. I had no more ammunition. Hum says, "I mean to get that caribou, I don't care what you do." Peter says, "If big one hurt very bad we git him in mornin'."

By time of sunrise we were all up. Hum got on his grub bag, shouldered his gun, and put right off. "We go on track big caribou," says Peter. "You take axe."

Leaving the useless gun, I followed Peter and we soon came to where we had routed the band. We followed the tracks and saw where they had stopped and then gone on in single file as they do when scared. There was one track much larger than any of the others. Strangely there was no blood, only a spot here and there. The Indian felt his way along cautiously feeling of the tracks from time to time.

"If he's hurt bad bimeby [by and by?] leave go by himself," and the Indian instructed me to keep clear on the outside of the tracks while he took up the other. We came to where they had lain down for the night and here were seven of them, round places melted in the snow.

We did not go more than three miles before as the Indian had predicted one large track separated from the rest and we followed that. We soon saw where it began to feed and were more mystified than ever. We had started into a thicket of small spruce when I saw the Indian, who was ahead, lift his gun. And as he fired I saw a dark form move away through the little trees. The bullet had struck a limb and had glanced.

Peter ran on and did not go a great ways when going down a gulch we saw on the other side the form of the caribou end-on, walking up the other. Firing, Peter never touched the caribou, and off [he] went again at a run. Peter now distanced me. When I got to him it was in open hardwood and I saw Peter, the caribou standing only thirty or forty yards off. I never knew a short-legged man like Peter could make snowshoes track so far apart. The caribou is end-on; Peter fires and the caribou only turns his side.

"Make sure, Peter, don't miss him," I called to the Indian. Peter aims again at the side. The caribou jumps at the shot and starts off at a lively run, a foreleg swinging. "Take axe," shouts Peter. "I got no more shot left."

I ran after the caribou and when it stopped I caught up and then it started again. Then I saw it sink down in the snow but every time it saw me it ran again. Then I saw it sink down at the foot of a large tree. I ran around so as to get behind the tree and when I thought I was near enough I struck with the pole of the axe. I missed and with a roar of fright the caribou sprang forward, struck me with its forefeet, knocked the axe out of my hands, and tumbled me over in the snow. I got up and shook the snow off and Peter simply roared. I picked up the axe where it had fallen ten feet away, but the caribou did not go far and I gave it a blow that put it out of its misery.

I never saw anyone so happy as Peter. "I never go yet but I git caribou."

When we came to dress the animal we found that the original shot had struck it behind the ears, had pierced the skin in two places, but had missed the back bone by a hair's breadth. It was simply stunned. "Now I show you how git meal Injun way. My father show me when I small boy in the woods." And Peter cut from the belly long strips of

Peter Joseph cooking meat, painting by Tappan Adney
(Dees Homer private collection)

meat, built a large fire, threaded the strips of meat on slender sticks and stuck them in the ground before the fire.

"Best way have some pork stick on top, run down makum taste better." There was no salt but that did not worry Peter at all. "I bin one time in the woods, kill plenty moose, three weeks no salt 'tall."

We cut up the animal, cut off some steaks, cached the meat in the snow. "Good chance black cat[2] come eat caribou meat."

It happened we were not far from a deserted lumber camp, on what is known as Thirteen Mile Brook and it is a good five miles to our camp. We are here on an old lumber road that leads out to the railroad, nearer home than the Ayers Lake camp.

Next morning we go back to the camp and find Hum just back. He had got after the other caribou and had given it a hard chase but had lost. He had stayed all night at the settlement. Hum agreed with us that it would be better to break camp and go to where the caribou lay and start home from there. It is after dark when we get to the old camp and to find the trail to the cache we have to strike matches.

We shoveled the snow off the meat, loaded it onto the toboggan. The woods were so dark we almost got lost. When we struck the lumber road some teams had been along and it was so rough we couldn't show-shoe and we couldn't pull the toboggan without them. It was very late when we reached the camp.

When we got all our camp stuff on the toboggan, the meat, and got the rope over the back of our neck we could hardly budge it. The wood shoes were not like steel and the toboggan sank far down.

Peter said, "We kin haul it all way in, not much heavy." Hum took it a turn then I took hold. It was about the toughest pulling I ever did. Then we made Peter get in the harness and he didn't pull it far before he said, "Guess mebbe leave um some longside the road."

We dumped off the two rib pieces and a fore quarter and covered them with snow. Then it was much easier. The road was a clean road, unbroken and level, through spruce lands.

Peter went on ahead. We took turns with the load but it was not a cinch. We had to haul on our snowshoes. We went miles but no sign of Peter. When we did come up with him we were a little cross. We made [him] get hold and then we struck for the end of the road. About a mile, we came to the end of it. There was a rail lumber camp by the railroad. We sat up and had [a] bite of warm beans and molasses and hot boiled tea like lye and felt fine. Poor Peter came in a long while after. I guess he had a hard time of it. After Peter got a bite Hum and I took hold of the toboggan, and we put it on the railroad track. There was not much snow there, but the sled did not sink in. With a stick through the rope we could jog along. We kept Peter in a good dog trot. It was eight miles from the camp to the river. Night came on and it was after dark when we got to the river.

It was past the time of any trains downriver, so putting the toboggan onto the smooth sled road, we kept on and then we took to the smooth surface of the river. It was three miles to Peter's shanty by the river's bank at Hardscrabble [Upper Woodstock]. The Indian was now far in the rear. When he caught up, there was a real tone of gratitude in his voice as he said, "Boys, I never git here haul that myself." I have thought since that we pushed the poor old fellow too hard, but in those days we were not accustomed to spare ourselves, and we thought he had tried to shirk. We forgot that he was a man old enough to be our father. Poor old Peter, they don't hunt caribou where he is now, and it is one long Christmas.

(We had an Indian tan the hide of the caribou. It was used for a sleigh robe and I have it now in my studio. I made a knife sheath out of the hind shank and lost the knife on Serpentine several years afterward.)

SECOND CARIBOU HUNT TO

NACKAWICK AND GUIMAC

RECORDING SOME HABITS OF
THE WOODLAND CARIBOU

JANUARY

1889

T. A. & HUM. S.

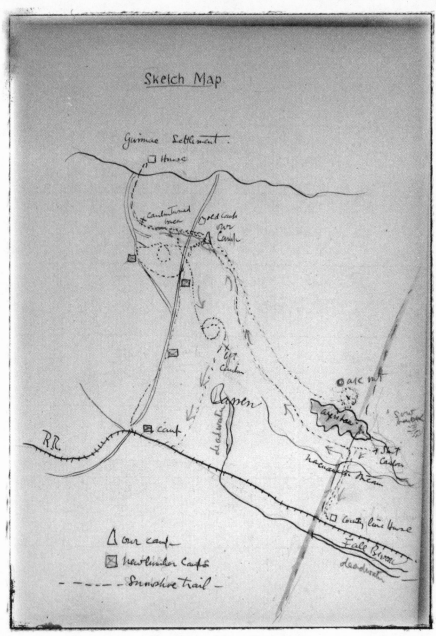

Second Ayers Lake caribou hunt

SECOND CARIBOU HUNT AND SOME IDIOSYNCRASIES
OF THE NACKAWICK CARIBOU

This was in every particular a chase. It was more that than anything
else. We learned some things about caribou that we but dimly realized
before. We have had ever since a profound respect for the woodland
caribou as he is found in the woods and barrens of Nackawick. We
had hardly been back two weeks from the last most satisfying, nay
satiating, hunt with Peter Joseph, that we yearned for the woods and
pelts of the caribou of the Nackawick Stream. We didn't get our fill
last and we thought how easy to do it again.

This time we made our own toboggan and shod it with iron shoes
two inches wide. We took a small tent and the usual provisions. Hum
had a wool blanket, I a cotton-batting comforter. It was the coldest
morning I ever felt. The dogs were howling with the cold and before
we had left Newburg far behind our breath had condensed in a rim
of frost around our caps, encrusting Hum's eyebrows and moustache
with frost and freezing my moccasins so stiff that I could not bend my
feet and would have frozen them but for three pairs of double-knit
wool socks of a thickness not understood in some more southern
climes. It was the kind of weather that the trees pop open.

We found a great change at the road where we had hauled the
caribou out. There were several new lumber camps on that road so
it was smooth walking on the hard glistening road. We got a lift on a
hauling team and went on in to Thirteen Mile Brook and deadwaters,
turned the stream, and picked out a bank where there would be
plenty of birch and maple wood and dry cedar, selected a place up
against a big yellow birch, and built a fire.

We built a fire where we wanted the tent — to thaw the snow and
ground — set up the tent facing the tree, piled the snow in around the

sides of the tent and a pole at the foot, made a bed of fir boughs and got ready for work.

The caribou were going to come right to us. We cleared a path to the deadwaters and with the axe chopped a hole in the ice for water. Having procured a fore shoulder of the caribou we had cached, we put some of that to stew, guns laid inside, snowshoes stuck heels down in the snow, mitten and socks hanging from the top of the tent pole drying. The frying pan full of pork sizzling over the fire completed the picture of a camp where we spent several days of the hardest winter weather.

30° below Zero Far[enheit]

We burned only the largest green logs we could handle and even they had to [be] replenished often. There is not much choice between beech, yellow birch, and rock maple.

1.   "Oh tamarack's a very good wood
      If you kin git it dry;
        But to make a fire of green tamarack,
      I'll be darned if I will try."

2.   "I'll go in search .
                of a big yellow birch,
    That's buried under the snow;
      Won't you tell me where it can be?——
    For I'll be darned if I do know."

The following morning we set out for Sewell's camp. Sewell's camp was nearly out as far as Hale's but he had a road of his own that connected with the road we came out on. Not caring to go so far around we endeavored to get there direct. It was spruce woods flat. It was snowing. We got lost, walked in a circle, at last found the camp, but did not know how to get back [the] way we came. Saw no caribou. We set out to return, being told Sewell's works extended within [a] quarter of a mile of the end of Hale's road. It was dark when we reached the end of Sewell's road. Hum went into the woods every now and then, calling so as not to get lost, came back, reported he could not find Hale's works; went back to Sewell's stayed all night. Next morning went over found Hale's works without trouble and then his camp and home again. No caribou.

There was probably two feet of snow now or more. Unlike the moose, the caribou does not yard but travels all winter from place to place, now on the barrens where the old men's beards[1] hangs to the scrub tamaracks and cat spruce, now on the hardwood ridges where they get the yew and especially do they congregate about the works of lumbermen, coming in the night time to feed off the tops freshly cut. That was why we thought the lumber works a good place to go for them.

The caribou is not affected by any depth of snow. Their hoofs are broad and spreading and they can jump, alighting on the gambrels, and get along at a rapid pace in snow where a moose or a deer would go up to its belly. I never knew but one case of a caribou being run down and it happened near a camp of the Gibson Brook east of Woodstock in a circumscribed area of forest and it so happened that the caribou so directed his course that each morning a fresh start could be made from the camp. It took three days to wear the caribou out.

A deer will step on the track that a caribou has made and if it [is] not frozen it will break through and the caribou is a much heavier animal.

We laid straight for Ayers Lake next morning and went to our old camp. Looking across the lake we could faintly make out fresh caribou tracks on the opposite shore.

Seeing that the wind was blowing in the direction that the tracks were leading, namely inland from the shore, we decided not to follow them but to go around so as to strike them farther on. We circled until we described a complete circle less than half a mile in diameter and came back to our tracks again. We had not passed a track going away. The caribou were inside of that circle.

There was no other way now but to follow the tracks as we intended, and now a peculiar thing happened.

The tracks we were on also began to circle about and presently we came upon four or five warm beds where they had just been lying in the snow. There were evidences of a sudden departure. The caribou had deliberately walked in a spiral and then lain down secure in the knowledge that nothing could approach on their track without their getting scent of it. They had scented us and were gone.

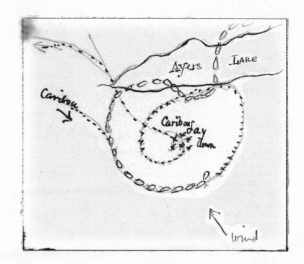

Caribou and
snowshoe tracks

We ran as fast as we could on their track. It led to the lower end
of the lake and then down below. It was now dusk which is practically
dark, in the woods. I was running ahead with the carbine and I had a
strap on it to carry by and we displayed no caution, being more intent
on getting even a flying shot then before dark, and I ran looking each
side the track [*sic*] when Hum, who was at my heels, shouted for me
to look and there right in front of me twenty yards off stood a caribou
looking at me. I raised the rifle but the strap covered the sight. I took
it down and the caribou moved and stood fifty yards off broadside.
The second shot hit it, Hum says, in the flank. The caribou jumped and
when I got there, there on the snow was a spray of blood. The caribou
was gone. Every little while was the spray of blood. But it was dark
and we had to give it up and struck for the section man's house at the
county line.

Next morning, as early as we could get up, we struck the trail
again. It had turned and was heading the way we wanted to go. We
came to where it had lain down but there was only that spray of blood
and soon even that ceased. We followed the track until we passed our
tent and then went on towards Guimac. It got dark and we had to

leave the caribou in a cedar swamp and we struck her down a lumber road three miles to the Guimac settlement where we stayed at a house.

When we got back we found that the caribou had turned around in the swamp and had taken our own back snowshoe tracks, which were now frozen solid, and made good walking. Again the caribou did precisely the same thing it did before. It circled and lay down to rest in the middle. Consequently we routed it again. It had had a good rest and now the third day was going as lively as at the start and was headed evidently striking back to Ayers Lake. We ran it till noon and then running upon the tracks of another band we gave it up in disgust and took after the fresh ones.

We did not go far before we came upon them in the thickest sort of place where there was no chance for a shot. The new band in their course ran over and passed within a stone's throw of Hale's camp. We followed them down into the wood a mile or so and had to leave them. We had discovered one fact about the caribou but we had yet others to learn. We returned to the camp at Hale's and stayed there all night.

In the morning we awoke to find a slight snow on the crust, that made the snowshoes noiseless. We regained the track and found where they had spent the night. There were eight or ten in the band. Hum was carrying the rifle. We had had such bad luck that Hum had left his gun, so today having the prospect of a shot I gave him the gun.

The Snider carbine, the arm that the Canadian artillery are armed with, has a peculiar breech mechanism. When a shot has been fired the shell cannot be extracted without cocking. When I gave Hum the gun I explained this to him and I said, "Hum, now I tell you you are going to get mixed when you go to shoot. I tell you now, for as sure as you are born it is going to happen."

When we came onto the fresh beds we excitedly pushed forward, Hum a little distance ahead. Suddenly I heard a faraway sound.

"Do you hear that?" I whispered to Hum. It came again, a curious yowl far off.

"Is that sound a man," I asked, "or a wolf?"

Hum gave no reply, for the third time it broke out near at hand, I can liken it to no sound but that which a giant tomcat might make. Naturally we were worked to a pitch of excitement.

Suddenly Hum became aware that a caribou was looking at him not thirty paces from him. Hastily jerking his gun to his shoulder, he fires. The caribou does not move. Hum tries to break the breech. It sticks because he has not half-cocked it. He tugs at it half a minute while the caribou stands gazing in astonishment. Then he throws the gun to me but too late — the caribou has started and as we run down to get nearer we hear a pump, pump at our right and two more caribou take off working their tails.

All thought of what we had heard went out of our minds. We never decided whether it was a Lucifer. Some men in the camp heard the same thing one night as they were returning to camp and not liking the sound of it they hurried to the camp. They thought it was an Indian devil.

We ran onto the track of the caribou. It began to swing and before three quarters of a mile they had circled entirely and gotten our wind and where we gave it up they were laying straight across the barren single file. Where they had gone through a snowdrift it looked like the work of a snowplow.

When running, the caribou drops in single file and where the work is hard, first one takes the lead breaking way and then he steps to one side and another takes [his] place.

We struck for the clearing, reached the railroad. We found it warm in the woods and our clothes were wet from the snow that fell from boughs but in the open a cutting wind froze our clothes until they were stiff as pasteboard and we could hardly walk in them. We went back in with a lumber team of Hale's.

We hadn't spent much time in our tent but one of those nights was not to be forgotten. It was intensely bitter. We piled on the logs till they roasted our feet, pulled our caps down over our ears, kept our mittens on, but even then we liked to have froze. One time I smelled something burning and got up and found it was my cotton quilt afire. I stamped the fire out and went to bed but pretty soon the fire had eaten another big hole. I got up and I spent the rest of that night trying to save the quilt but it lingered in the fibres of the cotton and in the morning that quilt was like a map of the Grecian Archipelago.

We thought it was about time to go so we packed our stuff on the toboggan again. A logging team going all the way in to the river was going our way so Hum got aboard the load of logs. We tied the toboggan rope to the back of the bobsleds and I got on the toboggan and rode all the way in.

We had learned several things about a caribou:

First, that when he lies down in a place where he suspects danger, he circles about so that nothing can approach, without giving their scent.

Second, when routed they may stand stupidly but when they start they circle to get the scent, and

Third, when they have once got the scent they take a bee line and get right out of that country and go to another range. It is no use running after them unless you know the course they invariably take and then you may be able to intercept them, as where they turn aside to follow a frozen water course.

SNOWSHOES

The best snowshoes are made of caribou hide. Caribou hide seems rather to tighten than stretch when wet.

Next best is yearling calf. Young calf (staggering bob)[1] is used for all small snowshoes and for heels and toes. Cowhide is used in the middles of cheap snowshoes. Also horsehide is used for this. Sheepskin is very poor but sometimes used for heels and toes. Moosehide is sometimes used but is usually made into moccasins.

The frame of the snowshoe is made of ash with cross pieces of maple. I saw beech used once for the whole frame but it is too heavy. The frames are bent while green. If the toes are to turn up the mated frames are tied together and a wedge driven between the toes to the required distance. Most of the shoes are turned up. Some prefer them flat, in which case after one side has got worn the shoe can be turned over and the other side used.

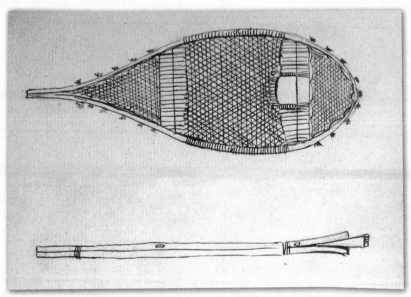

Snowshoe frame and turning the toes up

The Rawhide

The hide is scraped of the hair and soaked thoroughly. The filling of a snowshoe is called "babbish" (French word)[2].

"Babbish" is made as follows. The periphery of the skin is evened and a string or strap is started around about an inch in width and is continued around and around continuously. But this whole band is not cut at once. The first cut is made for several inches and then subdivided into strings a quarter of an inch or less in width. Then another large cut is made and the subdivision continues. These strings are cut wider, and from a thicker hide or part of the hide, for the middles, and as thin as the material will allow for the toes and heels, where not so much strength is needed.

The babbish is gathered into bunches and foot by foot twisted tight and pulled so as to take every bit of stretch out of them and then they are rolled upon sticks ready for use. From the very thickest part of the back [of the animal] a strap is taken to go across the shoe behind the front cross bar for a toe strap where the strain is in walking, especially when going uphill. And another is used to go over the toe.

An Indian takes a little roll of babbish into the woods to repair his shoes, or a piece of rawhide from which it can be cut.

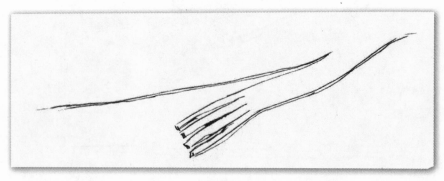

Babbish

In case of breakage, new bows[3] can be replaced without cutting the middles. The heels and toes are laced in and this lacing only needs to be cut and the old bow slipped out and the new ones slipped in their place, the heels riveted together again, and the toes and heels laced in again.

The Snowshoe Fastening

A band of soft tanned hide is best for this. There are three ways of tying this string:

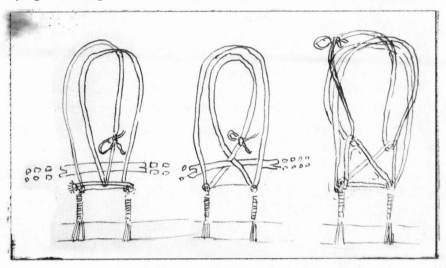

The snowshoe fastening

[Penciled note on reverse, added later:] (For protection, the bows are wrapped with leather and bottoms are laced with leather. Some snowshoes have two, instead of one toe strap, to balance the other.)

There is another way of fastening that has some advantages. It is a leather strap and buckle shown as follows:

I saw one very large and wide pair of snowshoes made probably in Montreal to order wherein the middles were laced in like the toes and heels instead of the rawhide going around the frames.

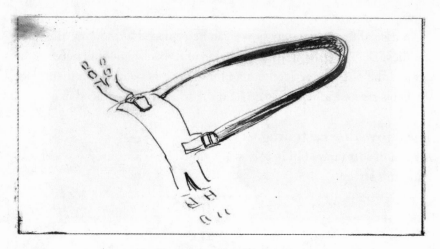

Leather strap and buckle fastening

At the points where a snowshoe wears it is well to lace in considerable leather, also to wind some around the frames in the middle. The life
of the shoe is prolonged.

Wet snow is hard on them and unless well made go to pieces.
Ash splints have been used to repair, even make some.

*Editor's Note: The following passage on snowshoes is transcribed
directly from Adney's handwritten copy, inserted separately into
the journal, and reproduced here on facing pages. It is a more
detailed version of the snowshoe-making description on previous
pages.*

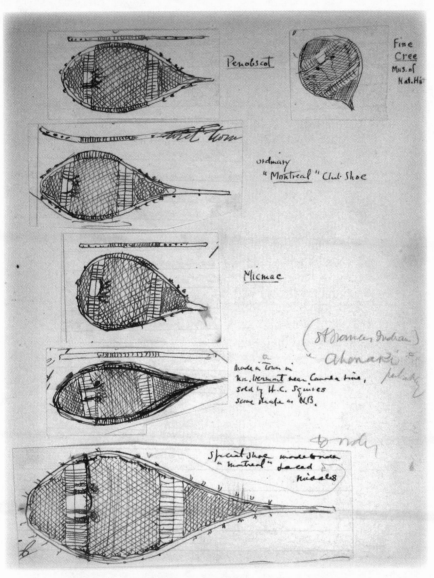

Penobscot

Fine
Cree
Mus. of
Nat. Hi*

ordinary
" Montreal " Club Shoe

Micmac

(St Thomas Indian)
" Abonaki "

made a Town in
Mn. Vermont near Canada line,
sold by H.C. Squires
same shape as N.B.

Special shoe made under
" Montreal " Laced
middles

Penobscot, Cree, Micmac, "Montreal," and St. Francis snowshoes

113

Frames White ash nearly always
Maple ~~crash~~ for crosspieces
(Beech reed (oak) for whole snowshoe)

Hide is scraped of the hair and soaked.
Then spread out and the edges trimed so as to make a
continuous outline.
One narrow threat is cut evenly for several inches
and the is cut same distance
until half a dozen ~~close~~ are cut the same distance.
Then the first cut is continued several inches more
then the next the same, and thus round and round
the hide, not cutting any one string all along
steady but taking along with you a bunch of half a dozen strings.
These strings are cut wider and of thicker hides
for the middle of the snowshoe and as narrow
and fine as the toughness of the hide will allow for
heels and toes.
These strings are then gathered in bunches and
twisted tight by means of stress and pulled and
twisted until the "stretch" elasticity is all taken
out then they are pulled upon sticks to for use.
From the very choicest part of the skin on the back, a
stout piece is taken out to be put across just behind the
front crosspiece, where the most of the strain comes
in walking especially climbing up hill

The bows are whittled the proper shape by
measurments and mortised in four places for the crossbars
the ends are then brought together and riveted with
a copper rivet or nailed. The crosspieces are slipped
in places as in diagrams.
If the toes are to turn up the two nailed frames
are tied together back to back and at the extreme
point of a ~~wedge~~ piece wood is driven between the frames which
holds the toes apart any distance that may be desired.
And the wood is allowed to season in that position

One advantage of flat snowshoes is that
when the rawhide has worn quite thin on the
lower side where it passes around the bows it can
be turned over and the unworn upper side used as

Snowshoes

Frames: White ash nearly always

Maple or ash for crosspieces

Beech used (once) for whole showshoe

The hide is scraped of the hair and soaked. Then spread out and the edges trimmed, so as to make a continuous outline. One narrow thread is cut evenly for several inches, another is cut the same distance until half a dozen, more or less, are cut the same distance. Then the first cut is continued several inches more, then the next the same, and thus round and round the hide, not cutting any one string among by itself, but taking along with you a bunch of half a dozen strips. These strips are cut wider and of thicker hides for the middles of the snowshoes, and as narrow and fine as the toughness of the hide will allow for heels and toes.

These strings are then gathered in bunches and twisted tight by means of sticks and pulled and twisted until the "stretch" elasticity is all taken out then they are rolled upon sticks for use. From the very thickest part of the skin on the back, a stout piece is taken out to be put across just behind the front crosspiece, where most of the strain comes in walking, especially climbing up hills.

The bows are whittled the proper shape by measurements and mortised in four places for the crossbars. The ends are then brought together and riveted (now) with a copper rivet or nailed. The crosspieces are slipped in place as in diagrams.

If the toes are to turn up, the two mated frames are tied together back to back and at the extreme front tip a wedge piece of wood is driven between the frames, which holds the toes apart any distance that may be desired. And the wood is allowed to season in that position.

One advantage of flat snowshoes is that when the rawhide has worn quite thin on the lower side, where it passes around the bows, it can be turned over and the unworn upper side used as (continued on page 117) underside. Thus the life of the shoe is prolonged.

Newbows may be inserted as before. This is done when in New Shoes a bow has broken. The toes and heels are ripped out by cutting the string with which they are threaded in place, and taking out the rivet at their end. ~~the~~ By pulling the crossbars are slipped only the mortises and the middle of the shoes are slowly worked off toward the back, and the bows are finally taken out. The new bows are put in by reversing the process. And finally, the toes and heels are placed in place to the new bows by a new string

For additional protection against the sharp cutting crust of spring. a string of rawhide is wrapped round and round ~~the bow~~ where the rawhide passes over the ~~bows~~.

An indian always carries a lot of rawhide things in his pocket or a piece of hide which he can cut up, for repairing breaks in the snowshoes, when he goes into the woods.

For additional protection at a spot that wears underneath quickest, strips of leather or things are wound over and over the spot where the ball of the foot and the toe rest

There always one narrow strap underwhich the tip of the toe is thrust. Sometimes there is another an inch or so farther back, which makes the tail of the shoe rise easily lifted when turning around quickly.

The string of cowhide or moosehide is tied in different ways

(continued from page 115)
underside. Thus the life of the shoe is prolonged.

New bows may be inserted as follows. This is done when in new shoes, a bow has broken. The toes and heels are ripped out by cutting the string with which they are threaded in place, and taking out the rivets at the end. By pulling, the crosspieces are slipped out of their mortises and the middle of the shoes are slowly worked off toward the back, and the bows are finally taken out. The new bows are put in by reversing the process. And finally the toes and heels are laced in place to the new bows by a fresh string.

For additional protection against the sharp cutting crusts of spring. A string of rawhide is wrapped round and round where the rawhide passes over the bows. An Indian always carries a lot of rawhide thongs in his pocket or a piece of hide which he can cut up, for repairing breaks in the snowshoes, when he goes into the woods.

For additional protection at a spot that wears underneath greatest, strips of leather or thongs are wound over and over the spot where the ball of the foot and the toe rest.

There [is] always one narrow strap under which the tip of the toe is thrust. Sometimes there is another, an inch or so farther back, which makes the tail of the shoe more easily lifted when turning around especially.

The string of cowhide or moosehide is tied in different ways.

In New Brunswick the snow shoe is laced
in this manner. The Toe-strap is placed
a little farther back than usual and thus
a leverage or grip is obtained for lifting the
snowshoe and throwing the heels around.
More control is given of the Snowshoe.
The lacing string is tied across the toe just
where the ordinary toe strap is placed.
Even when the ordinary toe strap is used, placed far
forward this style of tying may also be used

And when the front strap is worn the string
need not be unrolled as is worth while, as when
it is used instead of the Snowshoe proper

Again a snow shoe may be laced thus
And is a common mode
of tying the string

The Indians have
another way that
probably originated with

themselves. Somewhat in this manner.

A very large pair of Snow shoes
made of same shape as "Montreal" snow shoes
seen at Woodstock had the middle laced
in nearly the same manner as the heels & toes.
And were worn by the
man said to have the largest
feet in
New Brunswick

118

In New Brunswick the snowshoe is laced in this manner. The toe strap is placed a little farther back than usual and thus a leverage or grip is obtained for lifting the snowshoe and throwing the heels around. More control is given of the snowshoe. The lacing string is tied across the toe just where the ordinary toe strap is placed. Even when the ordinary toe strap is used, placed far forward, this style of tying may still be used. And when the front strap is worn the string need not be knotted so as not to slip, as when it is used instead of the snowshoe proper.

Again, a snowshoe may be laced thus and is a common mode of tying the string.

The Indians have another way that probably originated with themselves, somewhat in this manner. A very large pair of snowshoes, made same shape as "Montreal" snowshoes seen at Woodstock, had the middle laced in nearly the same manner as the heels and toes thus. And were worn by the man said to have the largest feet in New Brunswick.

The Common Moccasin worn winter and summer
may be be made of any stout leather even bootlegs,
or moose hide.
The tongues are cut out this shape:

A cord or string is passed around
the foot whose length equals the width
of the tongue plus the width of the
leather (see Note @ at the end
of the page

and the sole and sides are of one piece thus

Nor article
How to make
a moccasin
see Harpers
Young people
about Nov. 189

Then the edges of this
are crimped and sewed
to the tongue this

The sewed part is next
laid on a stone and pounded out
flat with a hammer in the seam
portion.

It is and given to the future wearer (when made to order)
and the toe is thrust up as far as necessary and
the ends are bent around back of the heel and marked
then the notches are brought together and the
leather is cut thus

The dew are cut off and if the
moccasin is to have a tail behind
which keep the snowshoe strap from dragging
of behind the cut is made thus:

Which when unfolded looks like this

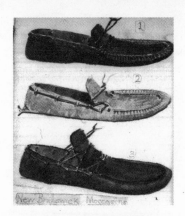

New Brunswick Moccasins

(Peabody Essex Museum Neg. No. 32080)

Moccasins

The common moccasin worn winter and summer may be made of any stout leather, even boot tops or moosehide. The tongues are cut out this shape:

A [illegible] or string is passed around the foot, where length equals the width of the tongue plus the width of the leather, and the sole and sides are of one piece, thus:

Then the edges of this are crimped and sewed to the tongue thus:

The sewed part is next laid on a stone and pounded out flat with a hammer in the same position. It is next given to the future wearer (when made to order) and the toe is thrust in as far as necessary and the ends are bent around back of the heel and marked. Then the notches are brought together and the leather is cut thus:

The ends are cut off and if the moccasin is to have a tail behind which keeps the snowshoe string from dropping off behind, a cut is made thus, which when unfolded looks like this:[4]

SECOND TRIP TO

NEW
BRUNSWICK

AND FIRST TRIP TO

NOVA SCOTIA

SUMMER OF

1890

SECOND TRIP TO NEW BRUNSWICK AND [FIRST TRIP TO] NOVA SCOTIA

I had been living but a short time with Edmund Collins and Bliss Carman[1] at the Old University[2] Building in Washington Square, when Collins suggested that we might take a profitable trip to Nova Scotia in time for the Exercises of the Centennial of Kings College at Windsor.

Adney on the roof of the University Building, Washington Square, New York City, about 1889 or 1890, age 21 or 22

We left New York together by Fall River boat, were joined in Boston by Dr. Farquhar Ferguson of the New York Hospital and Dr. Buchannan. Took steamer for Yarmouth, then train for Digby, then up Annapolis Basin in the little "Evangeline" to Annapolis, the train again through the famed Annapolis Valley past the dyke and meadows of Grand Pre to the old Town of Windsor on the Avon, the same that Charles Dudley Warner described when the tide was out as "an ugly gash in the earth."

Collins's friend Charles G.D. Roberts (Charles alphabet Roberts)[3]

We took rooms with Mrs. Mearns down by the far gate of Kings College and became a frequent guest at Prof. Roberts's, and I made a valued friend in Prof. Vroom of the Divinity.

Windsor, Nova Scotia

Here I met again Goodridge Roberts whom I had met on the *David Weston* going up to Fredericton when I first landed in the province. I spent a month about Windsor and Grand Pre and Minas Basin, when, college being over, I had a cordial invitation to visit Prof. Vroom and the house of the late Colin Campbell,[4] the home of his wife, at the mouth of the Weymouth or Sissiboo (Ak-sis-i-boo) River on the shore of St. Mary's Bay, an offshoot of the Bay of Fundy

There were the motherly Mrs. Campbell and the other daughter and with the presence of a young curate from Saint John we had all the material for a fine time. We had our own tennis court, a row boat, a thirteen-foot birch canoe, and a dog cart at our constant disposal. Inside the mouth of the Sissiboo the river widens and one arm ran in front of the house, which stood near the shore, and this arm had been converted by means of a dyke into a tide mill pond covering a few acres, and here were kept a number of fishing boats. There was a sandy beach in front of the house with the road between and we used to don a bathing suit and go out there each morning and take a dip in the bracing waters of the river.

Blomidon from Wolfville

Wishing you a very happy Xmas

F.W.

[Stroud]

Weymouth, Nova Scotia

The water was too chilly to stay in long. I used to go out to the end of the wharf and jump in head first and when I had swum ashore it was quite enough. There were flounders only a stone's throw from the bank and by going in the boats to the mouth of the river where the bottom was rocky and covered with eel grass, we could find all the crabs we wanted and now and then a lobster.

Sally port: Gateway of old French fortifications at Annapolis, N.S. In the distance are the old Officers Quarters, built by the British after its capture from the French. An old blockhouse has lately burned down that was built about 1650(?) and was the oldest blockhouse built in America. The old fortifications are almost the oldest, likewise.

Facing page: Blomidon from Wolfville [Christmas card from Professor Vroom]

Fish Trap

One day we resolved to visit a new fish trap five miles across the bay at Sandy Cove. We got a fisherman named Blackater, who owned a staunch twenty-two-foot sloop, to take the party across, consisting of all the family but Mrs. Campbell herself and two small children.

We got over to the trap all right and were just in time to see the men go out to the trap for the first lifting of the purse.[5] Before long it began to blow and we had a bad time. We went in a large boat having ten oars, a sort of a barge. We went inside the great purse. The gates were drawn up and the work of dipping out the fish began. As the net was drawn over the edge of our boat we began to see glints of silver and it was as if the whole sea were filled with the shining forms of myriads of finny creatures. With huge dip nets, dip after dip was made into the water and at every pull half a barrel of mackerel came out and then turned into the bottom of the boat, kicking and quivering, sending up showers of fine scales that got all over everything, our clothes and our faces.

When the boat was full, a great creature as long as a man and as big around as a beer keg was seen to be in the net. "A horse mackerel," shouted the fishermen, and with axe they went to work to kill it. Before they could get a strike it made a lunge and was through the net. They showed us one on the beach, one that they had killed. It had a smooth, leathery skin and the flesh is red and beefy.

When the boat was full, some forty barrels of good, fine mackerel, we went ashore, leaving the gates up, and the men went back later and took out enough more, they said, to make two hundred barrels. A schooner was there from Boston and as fast as they could, the fish were stowed into barrels to go to market.

The storm grew rapidly in violence until it was a thing not to be thought of to go back. The wind had full sweep up the bay and the waves grew higher than any I had ever seen before.

There was no room for us to stop at the fisherman's house, but several miles up the coast was another cove and a considerable village. There the greater portion of the party set out to walk while Blackater resolved to take the boat around by water. It is marvelous how these fishermen sail their boats within an inch of their lives. Their boats have no deck beyond a short cabin in the bow. The sides run up high and round, but when a wave breaks over there is no deck for it to wash off. It must every drop go inside and they are, every one of them, keel boats weighted with tons of stones and pig iron. If a wave ever got in they would go to the bottom like a shot.

We put out and it was a thrilling experience to me, used as I was only to the waters of Long Island Sound. The waves seemed to me like houses and we were going down the streets of a village. I have seen such waves since on the ocean. But we survived and probably Blackater would have thought nothing of it.

The Meanest Woman

We could not get all the way up to the town [in] our boat so we came up to the side of an old hulk that was moored at an equally old wharf. We went ashore feeling like shipwrecked mariners. We first looked around for a place where we could sleep so as to be near the boat and we picked out a likely barn but before turning in we thought of having supper.

Blackater hadn't a cent with him. I looked at [my] cash and I found some fifty-odd cents. We said to ourselves that will do for supper, the regular price being usually twenty-five cents each. We approached a house that had been pointed out to us as a place where they took mealers and I stated to the landlady the fact of our being storm bound and asked if we could have supper. Rather than have any misunderstanding I frankly told her the state of our finances and asked her if that would be sufficient. She said yes and proceeded to get our supper.

I shall never forget that supper. It consisted of tea, biscuit and butter, and ginger snaps. When we got through I asked her for the bill. I said, "'Madam, I have just fifty-three cents in the world."

"Well," she said, "I'll take the fifty-three." When I went to count it out I found only fifty-two cents and you should have seen the look on her face. I expressed to her, in the politest way I could summon, my exceeding great sorrow that we could not give her the amount promised.

That was, I think, the meanest person I ever met. We calculated she would charge us an even fifty cents. But evidently fisher like they must take everything in sight.

We slept in the barn on the hay and we did not ask anyone for fear of being charged for the privilege. A nest of newly born kittens somewhere under the hay enlivened the hours of darkness.

Next day we found the others and the sea had gone down sufficiently to be able to cross. We visited another trap near home where they drove oxen down into the water and unloaded from the boat into the cart. We likewise visited the French Shore and then after a month spent most pleasantly I went over to New Brunswick and up to Woodstock.

Got there in time for the races of the newly organized canoe club, took part in the race of the *Pocahontas* (birchbark) and the *Green Diamond* (canvas), and then went again to the deadwaters of the Gibson Brook with Hum, where we found the nest of a fish hawk with three eggs in a dead tree in the water, and coming back had a mishap with the canoe (canoe drifted loose across river). We went downriver, in as far as the old road.

After that, having been four months away, returned to Nova Scotia via Digby, visited Halifax and returned home with Collins via Intercolonial. In the same sleeper was Dr. Parker Morgan of New York. From Saint John we came all the way by train.

Soon left the University building and took up at the Winchester with Collins, Carman & co.

Canoe Races at Woodstock

The Canoe Club of Woodstock was in practical existence only during the month of August each year. That is because the Saint John River was full of ice during the winter months and full to the brim with water and saw logs rushing like a mill race at all other times.

At dead low water, however, the current subsides so that one can actually paddle all the way to Hardscrabble [Upper Woodstock], a stretch of two full miles. At hardly any time is the river unnavigable to the hardy canoeman who can stand erect in the light birch with the steel-shod pole, and fight the torrent, as the Indians do who go to the headwaters of these northern streams where the work is always past words to describe for arduousness. An Indian, or white men who have been brought up like them, no matter how sluggish the current, invariably use the pole and follow the shore when going up stream, for the speed is more considerable than that attained by the same exertion with a paddle.

But that style of work does not appeal to the ordinary town canoeman, who must take his outdoor amusements in a leisurely way, more especially when ladies share the work. So the paddle up the long stretch of nearly dead water was as much of real canoeing as most of the club cared for. But it must not be understood that all were like this. There were several gentlemen, members of former rowing clubs and gentlemen of athletic tendencies [and] tastes who were as good men in a canoe as one would find in the whole length of the Saint John River.

In the year 1892,[6] there was a revival of interest in canoeing. The year before there had been some canoeing and a club formed and they had a boathouse down by the river where a dozen or more canoes were stored. But this year there was more interest shown. The manager of the bank offered a trophy to be paddled for and prizes were offered for different races so it was resolved to get up a great race. The Major[7] got out all of his canoes. The customs collector[8] brought out a beautiful canoe painted green, not a birch but a canvas one.

The crews were picked out for the four-paddle, the two-paddle, and the singles, and there were to be races for Indians to take part in, and there was to be a novel race on saw logs to be participated in by the only ones who could do that sort of thing, some young men from the mills who were expert lumbermen and could cuff a log as only they can.

There were three rival crews in the four-paddle and there were a dozen entries in the singles, but the interest centered in the two-paddle race in which eight or nine canoes were entered. Of the barks there was only one which was conceded to [be] perhaps a bit faster than any, a beautiful craft, narrow and long and round on the bottom, of very smooth bark and bearing the name of its maker, P. Mitchell Jo,[9] who had turned out the best canoe an Indian was capable of building. This canoe was the property of the Major and it had just this much more interest to me that I was to handle the bow paddle in the Major's canoe.

All the canoe crews practiced assiduously, chiefly after dark when they were working for record. Herb and I got so we could fairly lift the *Pocahontas* through the water with the least perceptible side motion.[10]

The course was a float in front of the clubhouse upriver a quarter of a mile and return. There was an island in the river opposite the clubhouse and the main current of the river, which began to run swift at this point, ran the other side so at the start as the canoes would be ranged in line for the start, the water was dead and it continued dead all the way up the shore. But the Committee for some reason not understood by us fixed the stake boat out in the middle of the river. That was all right, but instead of letting the canoes wheel around from left to right as they naturally would they were required to turn the other way. That is, the canoe in the place of greatest disadvantage, farthest from shore, would be compelled by the swerve of the others out to go still more into the current while the inside ones would continue to be nearest the shore. It should have been the other way and that would have equalized things.

When the day of the race came, special trains came from nearby towns to witness the race and there gathered on the steep bank in front of the town where they commanded a clear view of the whole course, a great lot of people.

The contestants stripped down to lightest costume and I remember Herb and I had on a light shirt with the sleeves rolled up and a white handkerchief around our heads. We each wore moccasins. I had a six-foot paddle while Herb's was shorter, but wider in the blade.

We did not fear any of the other barks, but we were dubious about the *Green Diamond*, as she was called, the smooth painted canvas canoe, for the smoothest birchbark is not so smooth as painted canvas though we had given *Pocahontas* a good coat of shellac and she glistened in the afternoon sun.

The time came for the doubles and the seven canoes tossed for choice and as luck would have it the *Green Diamond* won the toss and chose the inside while we, having the very [last toss?], had to take the outside where we would have to fight the current. We had practiced the start until on the first push we could fairly lift the canoe out of the water and now we saw that our only hope was to get clear of the bunch on the start.

With muscles strained and tense, paddle blades just touching the water, we awaited the signal for the start. One, two, Go! The first jump we were half a canoe length ahead, then the rest recovered, got under way, and the scramble began, for a scramble it was. Herb's true eye and steady hand had her pointed straight for the stake boat but others were paddling like all possessed.

"Look out," we cried, but before we could swerve our neighbor bore down upon us, touched our gunwale, and not thinking in the excitement, the bow paddler seized our gunwale and pushed himself away, sending us back. While we were tangled the others got ahead and when we got clear we saw ahead of us every canoe.

"Take your time — be steady," spoke Herb in a quiet tone. I put my paddle in, in a way begotten on long practice, when I felt every ounce of width on the blade and I felt that there was no more power in the stroke.

By the time the first bark reached the stake boat we were rapidly gaining and had passed three canoes but our hearts fell when we saw turning the stake boat far ahead of all the *Green Diamond*, which had sneaked up the shore with no head current.

When we turned the boat, there were two canoes ahead and far ahead of them the *Green Diamond*. It was now a race between the *Pocahontas* and the *Green Diamond*. Could we catch them? Never before had I realized how strong Myles Moore was in the stern of the *Green Diamond* with sturdy George Baker in his bow. We had been paddling the same steady stroke and the *Pocahontas* was going like an arrow, not so much as a waver.

The crowd rose to their feet and shouted, "Go it, Herb, go it, Herb."

Herb rose on one knee half stooping and calls out hoarsely, "Now paddle." The *Pocahontas* fairly shot through the water. I saw only the distant boathouse and the form of the *Green Diamond*. At the cry of the crowd the green canoe had not spurted the way they had been spurting. The canoe rocked from side to side. There was no attempt to steer. They were bulling her home and I never saw the water boil as it did under the stern of the canoe. Myles was standing up. Could we catch and pass her? I never paddled as I did that time.

We were gaining on them fast. I could hardly hear the cheers of the crowds on the bank. I could hardly see the canoe in front. I only knew one thing, that my paddle was true across and that it was moving with all the quickness there was in human muscle.

We know what it is to be beaten. The *Green Diamond* crossed the winner, Myles and Baker pale and dripping, but had we one hundred yards to go more, the *Green Diamond* never would have won. The lead had been too much.

We had this much consolation, that what other canoes did not drop out at the turning point were not halfway down when we crossed the line, and also that [there] was some superiority in the model or materials of the canvas, that she won every race she went into that day. Even when it came to the Indian race, first choice took that canoe as the winning canoe. There was no crew that paddled so well together as we did and that we had clearly out-paddled the *Green Diamond*.

The log race was amusing and showed extraordinary skill. Three men entered. Each picked out a spruce a foot through, mounted it in sock feet so as not to slip, armed with a pole.

A greased pole over the water with a prize at the end proved even more attractive than the tub race for the boys.

(Baker was done for a hundred yards from the finish and Myles had driven the canoe in by sheer brute force. He had been lifting on handspikes[11] all summer in his father's mill and was as strong as a horse.) The prize was a handsome scarf pin for each [paddler] of the winning canoe.

THE SECOND TRIP TO GIBSON CREEK

Last July Hum and I got our heads together and planned a trip to a
place Hum knew where there were caribou, lynxes, otter, bear, and I
don't know what all. We got an old canoe, put in it what grub and stuff
we would need for several days. Our intention was to go half a dozen
miles below [Woodstock?] then take what was known as the Old Bull
Road to Four-Mile Brook, thence down to the Gibson Brook where
there was a dam and a large deadwaters and a small camp. Nights were
cold and we had to have a warm place to stay for we would have only
the little we could carry on our backs.

We dropped down the river, hid the canoe in the bushes, and started
in on the old road. It was plain enough at first but it had been many
years since any hauling had been done on it. It is always easier to follow
an indistinct path out, for all roads come together, but going in it is
usual for the roads to branch, and the road was so old and so grown.

Swam for the Canoe

When we got back to the river we found our canoe where we had left
it. The current was too swift possibly for paddling. Hum was good
in the canoe and all I could do was to help a little in the bow with
another pole.

There was a strong wind blowing upriver, kicking up a sea, but the
wind helped us along. We crossed over to the other side when in a tall
sand bank we espied the nest of a kingfisher.

We went ashore drawing the canoe up between two logs that lay
on the bank. It was fall driving time and the shores were strewn with
logs. I went at to dig the kingfisher out of his hole and Purps got down
to business on his own hook after a groundhog in the bank.

Happening to look out, to our dismay the canoe with all our stuff
was loose in the river but the wind had kept it from being carried

downstream by the rapid current and it was slowly being carried across the river and was now thirty or forty feet from shore. Without stopping to think twice I threw off my coat and with the canoe paddle I was digging with ran up the shore a ways and sprang into the water. It was cold as ice. I saw I would be rapidly borne down on the canoe by the current and with hard strokes I swam for the canoe, but I had not calculated on the swiftness of the current. I saw the trouble and with a desperate pull threw myself at the canoe, missed, and was carried by. I landed some distance below all wet and shivering. We held a war council and planned without delay. The bank was strewn with logs. Hastily pushing two small spruce logs into the water we got onto them straddle, Hum behind, I in front, our legs hanging down in the water to hold the raft together.

Then with all our might we pulled for the other bank. The river is some hundred of yards wide but we paddled so hard that when we reached the other side we were not a great ways below the canoe, which meanwhile had drifted to the other side and in the lee of the shore was also drifting. As the canoe came down we seized hold the gunwales and clambered in.

It was no trouble to get back and when we got to where we had left the dog we could hear only a faint sound down in the earth. Purps was after the groundhog and had dug under the bank so far that his voice could hardly be [heard?], wholly oblivious of the excitement we had just had. He never knew how near we came to having to walk all the way back home.

ACKNOWLEDGEMENTS

I would like to thank the dedicated and tireless people who helped me to interpret and illuminate Adney's occasionally murky original manuscript. Without their help, I would not have been able to edit, or indeed, understand it myself.

First and foremost is Jim Wheaton. His transcribed copy of Adney's original journal is the largest single contribution to this book. To Jim's existing work, supplemental additional text and images have been added to provide further background to places and events. Adney's original sketches have been restored to near-original condition.

Others helped with research or specialized knowledge of local geography, history, logging jargon, or Native linguistics. Greg Campbell, Librarian at the L.P. Fisher Public Library in Woodstock, provided invaluable research help on numerous occasions. Daryl Hunter of Keswick Ridge, NB, has been an indispensable supporter and contributor to my Adney biography work for years, and he provided invaluable review and editing help with this journal. Sally Polchies of the Woodstock First Nation also reviewed the manuscript with Daryl and helped with many corrections. R. Wallace "Wally" Hale provided interpretive help with logging jargon, gained from youthful experience working in sawmills. Pat Paul of the Tobique First Nation and Robert Leavitt of Fredericton, co-author of *A Passamaquoddy-Maliseet Dictionary*, provided translations of Maliseet words in the text. I want to thank all for their assistance. The text would certainly not be as readable or interesting without their contributions. Thank you also to Joan Adney Dragon, Adney's granddaughter, for granting permission to use the images of the canoe shoes (page 147) and the *Pocahontas* canoe (page 150) which were originally published in *The Bark Canoes and Skin Boats of North America* copyright © 1964 by Edwin Tappan Adney and Howard I. Chapelle. Reprinted by permission of Smithsonian Books.

I also acknowledge the great debt I owe David Gidmark, author and birchbark canoe builder of Maniwaki, Quebec. He introduced me to Adney during a canoe workshop and later gifted me his copy of Jim Wheaton's transcription of this journal. He also was the first to urge me to write Adney's biography. We all have turning points in our lives and people who played pivotal roles at those times. Looking back, I realize that David Gidmark was such a person for me on all things relating to Adney.

And finally, I want to acknowledge my wife, Liz, who has been my first and best reader and editor throughout my professional life as a writer. Her patient, loving support has sustained me all the years of our marriage and continues to do so today.

NOTES

Foreword

1   See Tappan Adney, *The Klondike Stampede* (1900; repr., Vancouver, UBC Press, 1994).

Introduction

1   For the rest of Adney's Maritime travel journals, see E. Tappan Adney, *The Travel Journals of Tappan Adney, Vol. 2, 1891-1896,* C. Ted Behne ed. (Fredericton NB: Goose Lane Editions, 2014).

First Trip to New Brunswick, 1887-1889

1   Trinity School was an Episcopal preparatory school (Headmaster, the Rev. Dr. Robert Holden), which Adney attended from September 1883 to June 1887. Trinity School was originally an offshoot of Trinity Church in lower Manhattan, one of America's oldest churches, chartered in 1697. When Adney attended, Trinity School was financed by contributions from Episcopal churches throughout Manhattan. Most students, including Adney, were the children of loyal Episcopal congregation members. Most attended as scholarship students, receiving the equivalent of a private-school education at no cost. Today the school is private and secular, no longer associated with Trinity Church. It has maintained its original emphasis on "classical" education (Latin, Greek, ancient history, ancient literature, etc.), and is considered one of the top five prep schools in the United States. Sources: Edward Stewart Moffat, *Trinity School, New York City: 1709-1959* (Ann Arbor, MI: University Microfilms, Inc., 1963); www.trinitywallstreet.org.

2   Fall River Line was the name of the company. It ran a handful of side-wheel steamboats that travelled by night between the docks along the Hudson near 30th Street in New York and Fall River, Massachusetts. Passengers would disembark in the morning at Fall River and then continue by train to Boston. One of the sidewheelers was a 110-footer named *Commonwealth*; perhaps the one Adney took on his first trip.

3   I think this is Adney's misspelling of the French word *distingué*, an adjective meaning "distinguished." Perhaps he was referring to himself as appearing distinguished to the women?

4   Adney doesn't say, but I assumed the Royal was a hotel where he had reservations. Note that he knew he was going to be staying for a week or so.

5   Adney was carrying letters to Montague Chamberlain (1844-1924) from members of the American Ornithologists' Union (AOU) in New York. Adney joined the AOU shortly after arriving in New York, at age fifteen, in 1883—the same year Montague Chamberlain co-founded the AOU. Adney first met him four years later, in 1887, around the time Chamberlain published *A Catalogue of Canadian Birds*. Both Chamberlain and Adney were contributors to *The Auk*, the quarterly journal of the AOU. Although Adney didn't know it at the time, he and Chamberlain would come to share another avocation, the ethnology of Native peoples, particularly the Maliseet people of New Brunswick.

    In 1899, Chamberlain published *Maliseet Vocabulary*, the first published substantial characterization of the Maliseet language, about sixteen hundred words. Many years later, the book was to become an important resource for Adney's own work on a comprehensive Maliseet grammar and vocabulary. Sources: AOU website, www.aou.org; and http://en.wikipedia.org/wiki/Montague_Chamberlain.

6   *oologist*: one who studies eggs.

7   George Edward Theodore Goodridge "T.G." Roberts (1877-1953) was a poet, novelist, and journalist, and the youngest brother of Charles G.D. Roberts, the celebrated Canadian poet and writer. When Adney met Theodore, the latter was ten years old and decades away from fame as a "man's" poet and novelist. He published thirty-four novels and more than one hundred poems and stories in periodicals. He was the father of the Canadian painter and art teacher Goodridge Roberts. His cousin Bliss Carman was another well-known poet and the editor of the New York magazine that published his first poem when he was eleven years old. Source: Nicola A. Faieta, "Theodore Goodridge Roberts," New Brunswick Literary Encyclopedia, http://w3.stu.ca/stu/sites/nble/r/roberts_theodore_goodridge.html.

8   Sir Charles G.D. Roberts (1860-1943) was a poet and writer known as the "Father of Canadian Literature." He was the first to express in his work the

new national sentiment following Canadian Confederation in 1867. He inspired and motivated other writers of his time, including his cousin Bliss Carman and Edmund Collins, with both of whom Adney briefly shared lodgings in New York in 1890. Sources: Thomas Hodd, "Charles G.D. Roberts," New Brunswick Literary Encyclopedia, http://w3.stu.ca/stu/sites/nble/r/roberts_g_d.html; M. Brook Taylor, "Joseph Edmund Collins," Dictionary of Canadian Biography Online, http://www.biographi.ca/en/bio/collins_joseph_edmund_12E.html

9   *deals*: antiquated term for piles of sawn lumber.

10 Francis Peabody Sharp (1823-1903), orchard owner and horticultural pioneer.

11 The "most remarkable house" was known locally as Sharp's Folly. It was built as a replacement for the large Victorian-design Sharp home that burned to the ground in 1881. The new house was a radical design for the 1880s, including a crenellated roofline that made it look more like a fortification than a home. It had many unconventional features including a gravel roof that leaked so badly the house became uninhabitable. It was abandoned and eventually collapsed. Source: Maude Henderson Miller, *History of Upper Woodstock* (Saint John, NB: Globe Printing Company, 1940).

12 Mary Ruth Adney, m. Charles Wyeth in 1900.

13 *Xenophon*: an ancient Greek professional soldier and writer.

14 Adney's first model canoe was rediscovered in 2007 as a result of this Adney notation. The story of how it was found is chronicled in C. Ted Behne, "Adney's First Model Canoe Rediscovered," *Wooden Canoe* 163:20 (February 2008). (*Wooden Canoe* is the bimonthly journal of the Wooden Canoe Heritage Association.)

15 "Milicete" is the spelling Adney used in the original journal. Years later, in other writings, he used "Malicite." Today, the preferred spelling is Maliseet. For the sake of consistency within the text, the spelling "Milicete" has been retained. Source: Website of the Union of New Brunswick Indians, www.unbi.org.

16 The Linnaean Society derives its name from the famed eighteenth-century Swedish naturalist Carl Linnaeus (1707-1778). His system of naming, ranking, and classifying organisms is still in wide use today. It is the world's oldest extant biological society. The Linnaean Society of New York was founded in 1878, just six years before Adney became a member in 1884, by a group of amateur

naturalists dedicated to ornithology and the natural sciences. Members now, as then, share a particular interest in the resident and migratory birdlife of the New York area. Source: Website of the Linnaean Society of New York, www. linnaeannewyork.org.

17 "Olastuk" is an alternative spelling to "Wallastook," the Maliseet name ("beautiful river") for the river renamed Saint John by colonists. The current spelling is "Wolastoq" and the Maliseet people refer to themselves as "Wolastoqiyik."

18 This is likely a reference to Rossiter Johnson, *A History of the French War, Ending in the Conquest of Canada* (New York, 1882), but Adney may also be referring to George Warburton, *Conquest of Canada* (2 vols.; London, 1849) — or he may be conflating the two.

19 The Wabanaki Confederacy was the name chosen by Native people in the Northeastern United States and the Maritime provinces of Canada for the alliance, around 1680, of five Algonkin-speaking tribal nations. These nations then and now are: the Abenaki of southern Quebec and northern Vermont, the Penobscot and Passamaquoddy of Maine, the Maliseet of New Brunswick, and the Mi'kmaq of New Brunswick, Quebec, and Nova Scotia. Source: Dr. Harald Prins, "Storm Clouds over Wabanakiak: Confederacy Diplomacy until Dummer's Treaty (1727)." Paper prepared for the Atlantic Policy Conference of First Nations Chiefs, Amherst, Nova Scotia, March 1999. Online at www. wabanaki.com/Harald_Prins.htm.

20 Adney calculation in the margin: "1887-75 = circa 1812."

21 Meductic was the site of a Maliseet fortified village downriver from the present Woodstock First Nation community, and about three kilometers above present-day Meductic village. Meductic was the eastern end of the Maliseet Trail, which led to Machias, Maine, and other parts of Maine, a four- to six-day journey via rivers, lakes, and portages. The famous seventeenth-century story of John Gyles, a Maine settler who was held captive for six years by Maliseet raiders, takes place partly on the Maliseet Trail and at Meductic. The original site is now submerged under the headpond of the Mactaquac Dam. Sources: G.F. Clarke, "The St. John River and Medoctec" and "Medoctec Continued," in *Someone before Us* (Fredericton, NB: Brunswick Press, 1968); Robert Cummins, "Imprisoned by Indians & French," www.friendsofmerrymeetingbay.org/mmb/ History/gyles.html.

22 Adney note: "Mûn-kw,d-_ik, buying, the whole occupation, place where."

23 Translations provided by Robert Leavitt, co-author with David Francis of *A Passamaquoddy-Maliseet Dictionary* (Fredericton, NB: Goose Lane Editions, 2009).

24 Some pasted-in drawings are missing here, and a page of the original is missing.

25 From *The Sharp Family* by Edwin Tappan Adney (1908), p.63: "Ziba Humboldt Sharp (5) Brother to Minnie Bell (5) born July 8, 1868; married Oct. 12, 1893, Mary; daughter of Alexander McKenzie, of Glassville, N.B., nurseryman and orchardist. About 1885 received from his father property on Sharp's Mountain, Northampton, where he resided. In 1907 he removed to Red Deer, Alberta, Canada, where he has founded a nursery business. Children: Mary Catherine, b. Aug. 29, 1894, d. Sept. 11, 1895. Olga Kathleen, b. Oct. 31, 1898. Norris John, b. Nov. 1, 1901. Francis Alexander, b. Oct. 1906."

26 Adjoining the Sharp property in Upper Woodstock was an iron works that had ceased operations in 1884. The property was later purchased by Sharp for use in his orchard and nursery business. In 1887, when Adney arrived, the only woods below the Sharp property were what the Sharps referred to as the "foundry" woods. A road ran through the woods, mostly used to haul iron ore from Jacksontown to the foundry property. Source: Edwin Tappan Adney, "History of the Foundry Property," Harriet Irving Archives, University of New Brunswick Library, Fredericton, New Brunswick.

27 *drummer*: refers to the sound male partridges make during territorial displays.

28 *Ox Bow*: refers to the Maine section of the Aroostook River, near the river's headwaters (near Oxbow, ME).

29 Modern-day spelling is Nackawic.

30 *Sow Back Mountain*: a small mountain, elevation about 305 metres, in northwestern Carleton County near Ayers Lake.

31 *Meduxnakik*: Meduxnekeag River, which flows into the Saint John.

32 *Guimac*: Becaguimec Stream, a tributary of the Saint John River.

33 *rails*: split sections of logs used in fences.

34 *peavey*: long steel-tipped hardwood pole for maneuvering logs on land or in water; *handspike*: a metal tool, similar to a crowbar in size and shape, for manipulating logs on a workbench or mill (see also note 11, page 151).

35 *horse yacht*: one of the rafts in tow, on which were kept stalls and feed for the tow horses.

36 Referring to the earlier conversation with "Old Margaret the Squaw." (Page 35)

A Trip in a Birch Canoe through the Squatook Lakes, September 24, 1888

1 The current spelling is Squatec Lakes.

2 A pencilled note specifies the tent dimensions as "6 x 8."

3 *sheldrake*: A large, crested, fish-eating diving duck, having a slender, hooked bill with serrated edges. Also known as Merganser.

4 Jim Wheaton included this passage from *The Bark Canoes and Skin Boats of North America* in his transcription to help readers better understand the somewhat obscure concept of canoe shoes to protect a bark hull from damage in rocky rapids. Both the text and the image are Adney's. Canoe shoes are an example of Native ingenuity and resourcefulness, which Adney greatly admired.

> The Malecite also fitted their river canoes with outside protection when much running of rapids or "quick water" work was to be done. This protection consisted of two sets of battens, each set being made up of five or six thin splints of cedar about 3/8 inch thick and 3 inches wide, tapering to 2 or 1-1/2 inches at one end: These were held together by four strips of basket ash, bark cord, or rawhide. Each cord was passed through holes or slits made edgewise through each splint. The cords were located so that when the splints were placed on the bottom of the canoe, the cords could be tied at the thwarts. The tapered ends of the splints were at the ends of the canoe; the butts of the two sets being lapped amidships with the lap toward the stern. This formed a wooden sheathing, outside the bottom, to protect the bark from rocks and snags or floating ice that might be met in rapids and small streams. The fitting was used also by the Micmac and Ojibway; it is not known whether this was an Indian or European invention. The French canoemen called it barre d'abordage and the Malecite P's-ta'k'n; the English woodsmen called the fitting "canoe shoes."

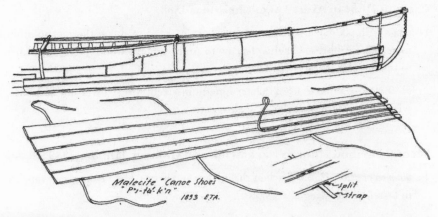

Figure 71

Reprinted from Tappan Adney, *The Bark Canoes and Skin Boats of North America* (Washington, D.C.: Smithsonian Institution Press, 1964), 80.

5   *scoter*: a diving sea-duck with dark, drab plumage.

6   Current spelling is Grand Touladi.

7   Fred Hale, brother of Juddy Hale, owner of a lumber camp.

8   Adney is not suggesting literally going over the falls. The water cascades over descending rocks and boulders at Grand Falls which might be crossed cautiously, carrying the canoe, to avoid the portage.

9   *Bumfrau*: Bumfrau Creek in 1888, now known as Bumfrow Stream, near Beechwood, New Brunswick.

10 This canoe race reference is significant because it dates the race prior to the fall of 1888, when the visit to the Squatec Lakes took place. Later in the journal, Adney mistakenly recalled that the race took place in 1892. He also had a memory lapse as to the color of the winning boat, calling it the *Black Diamond* here, but the *Green Diamond* later in the entry titled "Canoe Races at Woodstock."

Caribou Hunt to Ayers Lake, Christmas 1888

1 *Ambrose*: It is unclear whether Adney here makes a mistake; there is no other mention of Ambrose (likely referring to Ambrose Lockwood) being a member of the hunting party.

2 *black cat*: local name for a fisher, a medium-sized, forest-dwelling mammal, whose dark fur appears black against snow.

Second Caribou Hunt to Nackawick and Guimac, January 1889

1 *old men's beards*: *Usnea*, a lichen that grows and hangs down from tree branches in tassels resembling beards.

Snowshoes

1 *staggering bob*: English dialect for a very young calf.

2 French *babiche*; from Mi'qmaq *àpapìj*.

3 Adney uses the terms bows and frames to mean the same thing, the outer-edge frame of a snowshoe.

4 The accompanying sketch and continuing text are missing, having been cut from the original journal page. For more information on moccasins, see Adney's article "How To Make a Moccasin," *Recreation* (July 1905): 22-23.

Second Trip to New Brunswick and First Trip to Nova Scotia, 1890

1 Collins spent the following summer (1890) again at Windsor, Nova Scotia, visiting his friend Professor Roberts in hopes of reviving both his health and his literary career. Both were deteriorating, his health from excessive drinking and his career from lack of self-discipline. The visit briefly restored Collins's health, but ended his friendship with Roberts. He left behind a pile of bills for Roberts to pay. Two years later (1892), Collins's drinking finally killed him. His friend Bliss Carman (1861-1929) remained by his side until the end. Source: M. Brook Taylor, "Joseph Edmund Collins," Dictionary of Canadian Biography Online, http://www.biographi.ca/en/bio/collins_joseph_edmund_12E.html.

2 New York University is located near Washington Square in the heart of

Greenwich Village on the lower west side of Manhattan. During the late nineteenth century and up to the mid-twentieth century it was known as the Bohemian section of New York, home to writers, artists, and crafts people.

3   This strange incomplete sentence is taken verbatim from Adney's original journal. See notes 7 and 8, page 142-143, for more information on Charles G.D. Roberts and his younger brother Theodore Goodridge Roberts. See note 1 in this section about Joseph Edmund Collins, friend of the older Roberts.

4   Sir Colin Campbell was the Colonial Administrator of Nova Scotia during the 1830s. He died in London in 1847.

5   Purse seine nets are used to catch fish that aggregate close to the surface. The nets have floats at the top and weighted rings at the bottom, through which a rope is drawn to close the bottom of the net. The top and bottom of the net are pulled shut to trap the fish.

6   Adney's 1892 date in Woodstock is incorrect. The actual date, 1888, was determined by Greg Campbell, Librarian in the L.P. Fisher Public Library, Woodstock, New Brunswick, after examining local newspaper reports from 1888 to 1892. The only year that matched Adney's description was 1888. Since Adney transcribed his handwritten notes decades after the event, a memory lapse is assumed.

7   Major Herbert Dibblee, Canadian Army Reserve.

8   David F. Merritt is identified as the Customs Collector at Woodstock in 1888, in *McMillan's Agricultural and Nautical Almanac* (Saint John, NB: J. & A. McMillan, 1889).

9   P. Mitchell Jo is likely Peter Joe, Adney's Native mentor.

10 Adney's *The Bark Canoes and Skin Boats of North America* contains what may be a drawing of the racing canoe *Pocahontas*. Adney wrote in this later-published book of canoe research:

> One of the later developments took place on the St. John River, in New Brunswick, where two Indians, Jim Paul and Peter Polchies, both of St. Mary's, in 1888 built for a Lt. Col. Herbert Dibble [*sic*] of Woodstock the racing canoe illustrated above (fig. 66). This canoe, 19 feet 6-1/2 inches long overall and only 30-1/2 inches extreme beam, was of a design perhaps not characteristic of any particular type of

Malecite canoe, but it nevertheless shows two elements that may have appeared during the period of change in model . . . . This racing canoe is very lightly built and much decorated, the date 1888 being worked into the hull near one end.

Today this canoe is in poor repair, but preserved, in the Canadian Museum of Civilization at Hull, Quebec. It was donated in 2006, by Ian Bernard, one of the heirs of G. Frederick Clarke, who bought it from the Dibblee estate. Source: 2010 email exchange with Mary Bernard, sister of the donor, who lives in Cambridge, England, and who, like her renowned grandfather, is a published novelist.

Identification of this canoe as the *Pocahontas* is problematic since Adney's journal identifies P. Mitchell Jo as the builder of the one in the Woodstock race. However, this canoe is likely of the same design, very atypical of Maliseet canoes. Long and narrow, with a rounded bottom, modeled after a collegiate rowing shell, it would have been a very fast boat, moving in a straight line, but would not have turned well.

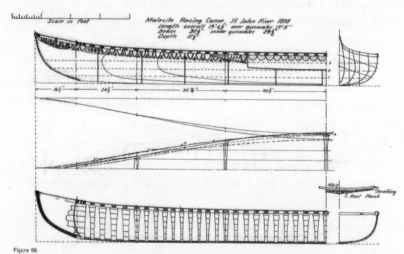

Figure 66

MALECITE RACING CANOE OF 1888, showing V-shaped keel piece placed between sheathing and bark to form deadrise.

Reprinted from Tappan Adney, *The Bark Canoes and Skin Boats of North America*

(Washington, D.C.: Smithsonian Institution Press, 1964), 75.

11 A handspike is a three- to four-foot iron bar used to turn a windlass, to roll logs up a slip into a sawmill from water level (but see also note 34, page 145). Two men stood on opposite sides of the horizontal windlass, around which chains holding the log were wound. The ends of the windlass axle were fitted with sockets, like empty spokes on the hub of a wagon wheel. Handspikes were inserted into the sockets and turned to haul the log sideways up the slip and onto the saw carriage for cutting. As each man removed a handspike to reset it in another hole, his partner would have to momentarily brace himself, taking the entire strain alone. The two had to work smoothly to prevent the log from slipping back. Or, if the windlass was ratcheted to prevent backward movement, it could be handled by one man, but he would have to be in very good physical shape, since the largest logs could weigh as much as a ton. Source: email exchange between the editor and R. Wallace Hale, Woodstock, New Brunswick, Dec. 2, 2009. (Hale worked for a time in a Woodstock sawmill when he was a preteen.)

INDEX

A

Abenaki 144
Acadia 31, 32
"Adney's First Model Canoe
    Rediscovered" 143
alder 43, 49, 54, 71, 72, 74, 76
Alexander, Joe 32
Alexander, Ned 32
Algonkin 144
American Ornithologists' Union
    (AOU) 142
Annapolis NS 124, 127
Annapolis Basin 124
Annapolis Valley NS 124
Aroostook River 61, 64, 85, 145
Art Students League 12
ash 76, 109, 112
Atalagwauktum 35
Athens OH 12
Auk, The 142
Avon River 125
Ayers Lake 87-89, 97, 100, 104, 106,
    145

B

babbish 110
Baker, George 52, 53, 60, 61, 134,
    135
Baker, Mrs. Samuel 52, 53, 57
Banks (oologist) 21
*Bark Canoes and Skin Boats of North
    America, The* 14, 146, 149
Bay of Fundy 21, 22, 125

bear 37-39, 43, 45, 47, 55, 57, 59,
    60, 68, 91, 136
    black 35, 60
Beardsley Brook 71
beaver 33, 38, 73
Becaguimec Stream 91, 99, 105, 145
beech 103, 109
Beechwood NB 147
Bernard, Ian 150
Bernard, Mary 150
birch 43, 71, 73, 75, 76, 101, 103,
    131, 132
    white 70
Black Diamond 86, 147
Blackater (fisherman at Sandy Cove
    NS) 128, 129
blackfly 68
Boston MA 19, 124, 128, 141
Bragdon, Jerry "Long Jerry" 59-60
Buchannan, Dr. 124
bulrushes 75, 77
Bumfrow Stream 85, 147

C

Caldwell, Davy 53, 55
Cambridge England 150
Campbell, Colin 125, 149
Campbell, Greg 139, 149
Campbell, Mrs. 125, 128
Campobello NB 20
Canadian Army Reserve 150
Canadian Museum of Civilization 150
canoes 29, 30, 31, 53, 55, 60-62, 64,

67, 68, 70-74, 76-78, 80, 82-86,
125, 130-137, 139, 146, 149-151
  birchbark 14, 15, 25, 27, 33, 62,
    65, 130, 133, 139
  canvas 130, 133
  Maliseet 150, 151
  model 16, 143
  shoes 146, 147
Cape Breton NS 28
caribou 28, 38, 43, 47, 48, 81, 87-95,
  97-109, 136
Carleton County 145
Carman, Bliss 124, 130, 142, 143,
  148
Catalogue of Canadian Birds, A 142
cedar 22, 33, 38, 39, 72, 74, 77, 101,
  106
Central Park, New York NY 12
Chamberlain, Montague 21, 22, 142
Chapel Hill NC 12
Chase, William Merritt 12
chokecherry 35, 76
chub 75
Clarke, G. Frederick 15, 150
Collins, Joseph Edmund 124, 125,
  130, 143, 148, 149
Columbia University 11, 23
Commonwealth 141
Connell, Allison 25
crab 127
cranberry 76
crow 22, 55
cusk 77

D

David Weston 22, 125
deer 23, 43, 104
Denys, Nicolas 28
Dibblee, Herbert 53, 131-134, 149
Digby NS 124, 130
duck 47, 48, 49, 71, 72, 146
  black 47
  sheldrake 69, 71
  white-winged scoter 75, 147

E

eagle
  bald 48, 49
Eagle River 76
Eastport ME 19-21
Edmundston NB 68
Eel River NB 59
elm 72, 76
  American 74
Evangeline NS 124

F

Fall River Line 141
Fall River MA 141
Ferguson, Dr. Farquhar 124
fir 20, 76, 102
First Peoples 9, 11, 14, 23, 27, 32
  children 33
fish traps 128
flagroot 35
Florenceville NB 85
flounder 20, 127
Four Mile Brook 43, 136
fox 43
Francis, David 145

Fredericton NB 22, 23, 26, 31, 35,
    51, 125, 139

G

Gaspe QC 28
Gibson Brook 43, 104, 130, 136
Gibson Creek 48, 136
Gibson Deadwaters 43-44
Gidmark, David 139
Gittis (lumber camp) 49
Gittis (person known as) 49
Giverson (log driver on Aroostook R.)
    61
Glassville NB 145
Gluskap 31
goose 58
Grand Falls 28-29
Grand Falls NB 26, 84
Grand Manan NB 20
Grand Pré NS 125
Grand Touladi Lake 76-78, 147
Grand Touladi River 78
Green, Henry 39
Green Diamond 130, 133-135, 147
Greenwich Village NY 149
Griffin (hauler near Mud Lake) 70, 81
groundhog 35, 37, 40, 42, 43, 136,
    137
gull 20
Gyles, John 144

H

Hale, Fred 50, 147
Hale, Juddy 50, 52, 147
Hale, R. Wallace Wally 139, 151
Hale's camp 103, 106, 107

Halifax NS 130
hawk
    fish 130
    sharp-shinned 22
Hayden family 54-55
Hayden's mill 55
hazelnut 35
Hebert, Felix 68
heron
    great blue 47, 49
Holden, Robert 141
horse
    Madawaska 70
houses
    birchbark 25, 28
Hudson River 141
Hull QC 150
Hunter, Daryl 139

I

Ike, "Black Ike" 55, 57
International Steamship Company 19
Inuit 28
I-so-ma-gwess-sis 33

J

Jack, Edward 31
Jacksontown NB 145
Joe, Gabe. *See* Joseph, Gabriel
Joe, Peter. *See* Joseph, Peter
John (horse) 43
Joseph, Gabriel 32, 89
Joseph, Peter 25, 28, 32, 87, 89-95,
    97, 98, 101, 132, 149-150

K

Keswick Ridge NB 139
kingfisher 136
Kings College 124-125
Klondike Stampede 9

L

L.P. Fisher Public Library 139, 149
Lane's Creek NB 25
Laporte, Jack 32
Laporte, Joe 32
Laporte, Mitchel (or Misel) 32
Leavitt, Robert 139, 145
Leland, N.E. 31
Linnaean Society 26, 143, 144
Linnaeus, Carl 143
Little Falls 67, 70
Little Falls NB 81, 83
lobster 127
Lockwood, Ambrose 27, 32, 91
Lolar, Gabe 32
Long Island Sound 129
loon 72, 75
lynx 43, 136

M

Machias ME 144
mackerel 128
Mactaquac dam 144
Madawaska River 68, 69, 81
Maliseet 13, 14, 26, 28, 30, 31, 139,
    142-144, 146
    dictionary 14
    grammar 142
    language 14, 142
    vocabulary 142

Maliseet Trail 144
Maliseet Vocabulary 142
Manawagonish (Meagone) Island NB
    22
Manhattan NY 141, 149
Maniwaki QC 139
maple 73, 101, 109
    rock 103
Mapleton NB 55
Margaret, "Old Margaret the Squaw"
    35, 64, 146
Mariners' Museum 15
Mattawamkeag ME 26
McKenzie, Alexander 145
Mearns, Mrs. 125
Meductic NB 29, 144
Meduxnekeag River 55, 56, 145
Merritt, David F. 149
Micmac *see* Mi'kmaq
Mi'kmaq 26, 28, 31, 144, 147
Mikmaq *see* Mi'kmaq
Miller, Maude Henderson 143
Minas Basin 125
mink 43
Missoula MT 59
moccasins 27, 63, 68, 101, 109, 121,
    133, 148
    moosehide 53, 121
Mohawk 26-31
Moliskus 35
Montreal QC 111
Moore (mill owner) 60
Moore, Myles 134-135
Moore's mill 60
moose 28, 31, 43, 97, 103
Morgan, Parker 130

mosquito 68
Mud Lake 70
Muin 35
Mûn-kwād-ĭk 31, 145
Munquot NB 31
Museum of Natural History 25
muskrat 55, 67

N

Nackawic NB 13, 49, 53, 54, 99, 101,
    145
Nackawic Stream 89, 101
Na-na-mik-tcis 33
Natural History Society (NY) 22
New York NY 11, 12, 14, 19, 22, 25,
    26, 124, 130, 141-144, 149
New York Hospital 124
New York University 148
Newburg NB 101
Newport News VA 15
Northampton NB 145
Notre Dame du Lac QC 78

O

Ohio University 12
Ojibway 147
Olastuk 28, 29, 144
Old Town ME 26
otter 43, 136
owl 39
    saw-whet 55
Oxbow ME 37, 145

P

partridge 33, 37, 40, 45, 47, 49, 70,
    75-78, 81

Passamaquoddy 26, 144
Passamaquoddy-Maliseet Dictionary, A 145
Paul, Jim 149
Paul, Noel (or Newell) 32, 35
Paul, Pat 139
Paul, Peter 14-15
Penobscot 26, 144
Perley, Francis 32, 64
petrel 19
Pittsboro NC 12
Pocahontas 86, 130-134, 149, 150
po-kwi-snau-i-es-sis 33
Polchies, Peter 149
Polchies, Sally 139
pollock 20
poplar 69, 75
porcupine 45-46
Portland ME 19-20
Presque Isle ME 37
Prins, Harald 144
Purps 37, 40-46, 68, 72, 75, 86, 136,
    137

Q

Queen Hotel 23

R

rabbit 35
Red Deer AB 145
redstart 20
Ring, John 50
Roberts, Charles G.D. 23, 31, 125,
    142, 143, 148
Roberts, Theodore Goodridge 22,
    125, 142, 149

S

Sabattis (or St. Baptiste) 32
sable 43
Saint John NB 19, 20, 22, 85, 125, 130
Saint John River 13, 19, 26, 28, 83, 131, 145, 149
Saint John Sun 31
Sally, Old 61
salmon 29, 33, 35, 37
sandpiper
  spotted 33
Sandy Cove NS 128
Sapier, Noel (or Newel[l]) Francis "Madewess" 28, 29, 32
sculpin 20
Serpentine River 98
Sewell's camp 103
Sharp, Francis Alexander 145
Sharp, Francis Peabody 143
Sharp, Humboldt 36-40, 43, 45, 47-50, 52, 67, 68, 72, 80, 82, 86, 87, 89, 92-94, 97-99, 101, 103, 105-108, 130, 136, 137, 145
Sharp, Mary Catherine 145
Sharp, Mary (McKenzie) 145
Sharp, Minnie Bell (Adney) 145
Sharp, Norris John 145
Sharp, Olga Kathleen 145
Sharp family 11, 23, 49, 52, 61, 143, 145
Sharp's Folly 143
Sharp's Mountain 145
sheepskin 53
Skinosis 35
Slipp, Whit 57-60
Slipps Store 57

Smith, Dr. 52
snowshoes 13, 27, 53, 90, 91, 95, 97, 98, 102, 105, 106, 109-112, 115, 117, 119, 121, 148
  Cree 113
  Mi'kmaq 113
  Montreal 113, 119
  Penobscot 113
  St. Francis 113
Solis, John 25, 32
Sow Back Mountain 53, 89, 91, 145
sparrow
  chipping 20
  savannah 22, 35
Sprague, Dr. 52
spruce 13, 22, 43, 73, 76, 90, 97, 103, 104, 135
  white 73
Squatec Lakes QC 13, 65, 67, 73, 75, 76, 146, 147
Squatook Lake *see* Squatec Lakes QC
Squatook River 72
squirrel 35, 37, 40
St. Mary's Bay 125
St. Marys NB 149
Stairs, Johnny 58
Stickney, Mr. 53
Stickney NB 53
Stickney's Mill 53
strawberry 35
Sulsulsili 35
Sunbury County NS 31
swallow 19
  bank 13, 23
  barn 13

T

tamarack 103, 104
Temiscouata Lake 78
Temiscouata Railroad 68
tern 20
Thirteen Mile Brook 97, 101
thrush
    hermit 22, 35
Tobique First Nation 139
Tobique Narrows NB 84
Tobique River 26, 63, 64, 84, 85
toboggans 82, 89, 90, 97, 98, 101,
    108
tomahawks 30
traps 38, 78, 89
Trinity Church 141
Trinity School 11, 141
trout 33, 37, 43, 50, 73, 75, 78, 81,
    89
turkey 58

U

Union of New Brunswick Indians 143
University of North Carolina 12
Upper Corner NB 62
Upper Woodstock NB 11, 16, 23, 61,
    86, 98, 131, 145

V

Vanwart 58
vireo
    red-eyed 20
Vroom, Professor 125

W

Wabanaki Confederacy 144
warbler
    bay-breasted 21
    Cape May 21
Warner, Charles Dudley 125
Washington and Jefferson College 12
Washington PE 12
Weymouth NS 127
Weymouth River 125
Wheaton, Jim 13, 139, 146
widgeon
    American 35
wigwams 33
willow 69
Windsor NS 23, 124, 125, 148
wolf 107
Wooden Canoe 143
Wooden Canoe Heritage Association
    143
Woodstock First Nation 14, 139
Woodstock NB 10, 14, 19, 23, 25, 29,
    30, 35, 48, 52, 54, 55, 56, 62, 64,
    84, 104, 119, 130, 131, 136, 139,
    144, 149, 150, 151
Wyeth, Charles 143
Wyeth, Mary Ruth (Adney) 11, 143

Y

Yarmouth NS 124
yellowthroat
    Marlyand 20